Lecture Notes
in Business Information Processing

386

More information about this series at http://www.springer.com/series/7911

Nicolas Herbaut · Marcello La Rosa (Eds.)

Advanced Information Systems Engineering

CAiSE Forum 2020
Grenoble, France, June 8–12, 2020
Proceedings

 Springer

Editors
Nicolas Herbaut🄳
Université Paris1 Panthéon-Sorbonne
Paris, France

Marcello La Rosa🄳
University of Melbourne
Melbourne, VIC, Australia

ISSN 1865-1348   ISSN 1865-1356 (electronic)
Lecture Notes in Business Information Processing
ISBN 978-3-030-58134-3   ISBN 978-3-030-58135-0 (eBook)
https://doi.org/10.1007/978-3-030-58135-0

This Springer imprint is published by the registered company Springer Nature Switzerland AG
The registered company address is: Gewerbestrasse 11, 6330 Cham, Switzerland

Preface

The objective of the CAiSE conference series is to provide a platform for the exchange of experience, preliminary research results, and ideas between the research community and industry in the field of information systems engineering. Over almost three decades, the conference has become the annual worldwide meeting point for the information system engineering community. This year, the 32nd edition of the CAiSE conference was organized by the Laboratory of Informatics of Grenoble (LIG) at Université Grenoble Alpes (UGA), France. However, due to the COVID-19 outbreak, it was held online during June 8–12, 2020.

The CAiSE Forum is one of the traditional tracks of the CAiSE conference. Intended to serve as an interactive platform, the Forum aims to present emerging new topics and controversial positions, as well as act as a platform for researchers to demonstrate innovative software tools and their applications. The CAiSE Forum sessions facilitate the interaction, discussion, and exchange of ideas among presenters and participants. In accordance, two types of submissions were called to the Forum this year:

- Visionary papers presenting innovative research projects, which are still at a relatively early stage of maturity, and do not necessarily include a full-scale validation.
- Demo papers describing innovative software tools that implement the results of research efforts. The tools and prototypes are presented as demos at the Forum.

Each submission was reviewed by three Program Committee (PC) members. Only those submissions for which there was an agreement on their relevance, novelty, and rigor were accepted for presentation at the Forum. Additionally, some papers were invited to the Forum as a result of the evaluation process in the CAiSE main research track. Altogether, 12 papers were accepted for presentation, out of a total of 19 submissions. The accepted papers are collected in this volume. These papers were presented via live online sessions. The authors also recorded a short video to summarize the key points of their contributions.

We would like to thank everyone who contributed to the CAiSE 2020 Forum. In particular, we thank the PC members for their reviews and help to promote the event, and the conference's PC chairs, Eric Yu and Schahram Dustdar, for their assistance with handling the papers coming from the main research track. We also thank all the authors for sharing their work with the community. Last, a big thank you goes to the CAiSE 2020 general chairs, Dominique Rieu and Camille Salinesi, and the Local Organizing Committee led by Agnes Front, for their remarkable support, especially during the troubled times of the COVID-19 outbreak.

June 2020

Nicolas Herbaut
Marcello La Rosa

Organization

Program Committee

Said Assar	Institut Mines-Télécom Business School, France
Saimir Bala	WU Vienna, Austria
Marco Comuzzi	Ulsan National Institute of Science and Technology, South Korea
Dolors Costal	Universitat Politècnica de Catalunya, Spain
Jose Luis de la Vara	University of Castilla-La Mancha, Spain
Chiara Di Francescomarino	Fondazione Bruno Kessler, IRST, Italy
Samuel A. Fricker	Blekinge Institute of Technology, Sweden
Giancarlo Guizzardi	Ontology and Conceptual Modeling Research Group (NEMO), Federal University of Espirito Santo (UFES), Brazil
Christos Kalloniatis	University of the Aegean, Greece
Dimka Karastoyanova	University of Groningen, The Netherlands
Daniel Lübke	Leibniz Universität Hannover, Germany
Fabrizio Maria Maggi	Free University of Bozen-Bolzano, Italy
Selmin Nurcan	Université Paris 1 Panthéon-Sorbonne, France
Michalis Pavlidis	University of Brighton, UK
Luise Pufahl	TU Berlin, Germany
Jolita Ralyté	University of Geneva, Switzerland
David Rosado	University of Castilla-La Mancha, Spain
Arik Senderovich	Technion, Israel
Arnon Sturm	Ben-Gurion University, Israel
Gianluigi Viscusi	EPFL-CDM-CSI, Switzerland
Monica Vitali	Politecnico di Milano, Italy
Moe Thandar Wynn	Queensland University of Technology, Australia

Contents

Flexible Integration of Blockchain with Business Process Automation: A Federated Architecture

Michael Adams[1]([✉]), Suriadi Suriadi[1], Akhil Kumar[2],
and Arthur H. M. ter Hofstede[1]

[1] Queensland University of Technology, Brisbane, Australia
{mj.adams,s.suriadi,a.terhofstede}@qut.edu.au
[2] Smeal College of Business, Penn State University, University Park, USA
akhil@psu.edu

Abstract. Blockchain technology enables various business transactions to be performed in an immutable and transparent manner. Within the business process management community, blockchain technology has been positioned as a way to better support the execution of inter-organisational business processes, where the entities involved may not completely trust each other. However, the architectures proposed thus far in the literature for blockchain-enabled business process management can be described as "heavy-weight", since they promote the blockchain platform as the monolithic focal point of all business logic and process operations. We propose an alternative: a federated and flexible architecture that leverages the capabilities of blockchain, but without overloading the functionalities of the blockchain platform with those already extant in Business Process Management Systems (BPMSs). We illustrate its benefits, and demonstrate its feasibility, through the implementation of a prototype.

Keywords: Blockchain · Process flexibility · Business process automation · Business process management systems

1 Introduction

A blockchain is a tamper-proof, replicated and distributed ledger [10] to which multiple parties can append transactional records in such a way that modification is prevented, in a technically-enforceable manner. Blockchain technology effectively guarantees that transactions, once recorded, become immutable [17], facilitating the execution of transactions across multiple, potentially untrusted parties without the need for a trusted intermediary. Naturally, blockchain opens up new opportunities to support the execution of cross-organisational business processes (i.e. those processes that necessitate interactions involving multiple discrete players) typically seen in many domains, such as supply chain management and manufacturing.

© Springer Nature Switzerland AG 2020
N. Herbaut and M. La Rosa (Eds.): CAiSE Forum 2020, LNBIP 386, pp. 1–13, 2020.
https://doi.org/10.1007/978-3-030-58135-0_1

In recent years, the Business Process Management (BPM) community has investigated ways to exploit blockchain for secure, cross-organisational process execution (see [6–8,19] for some initial approaches). In this paper, we specifically focus on the alternative architectural designs that integrate blockchain technologies with business process management systems (BPMS) to support process executions involving multiple, independent parties. We call such a system a *blockchain-integrated BPMS*.

A prominent architecture proposed for blockchain-integrated BPMS transforms a business process, expressed as one or more process models, into smart contracts (programmable transactions) that are then executed entirely upon a blockchain platform [6,19]. That is, all business rules, branching logic, instance data, resource allocation, access authorisations and process state management is deployed to and handled by the blockchain platform. Thus, the focal point of this architecture resides in the blockchain and the different parties involved in the business process must interact directly with this blockchain, both during process design time and runtime executions. We shall refer to such an architecture as *blockchain-centric*.

While blockchain-centric architectures may be appealing for some business process applications, and under certain threat assumptions and/or risk scenarios, it is not a universal solution. It is a *heavy-weight* architecture, with a rigidity that may not be necessary, or even desirable, in many other business process applications, for example where interactions between multiple parties are loosely-coupled and/or may involve asynchronous-type interactions. A heavy-weight architecture also overloads a blockchain system with a host of supporting compilers, components and mechanisms required to wholly accommodate business process design and execution within a distributed ledger. In effect, this tight integration necessitates a *duplication* of the capabilities that already exist within core execution engines of BPMSs.

Hence, we propose an alternative *federated* architecture, that is more decentralised, cooperative, and flexible, simpler to realise and better suited to meet the needs of a wide variety of cross-organisational settings. The proposed architecture allows component parts to each perform their fit-for-purpose capabilities in a federated whole, rather than overloading components with functionalities that are better performed by others. This architecture is flexible in that it is not tied to any particular type of blockchain platform or BPMS. It supports the minimisation of append operations to a blockchain, which are known to be resource-intensive [18,21], and does not require the creation and propagation of multiple smart contracts per execution instance.

This paper is structured as follows: a background discussion and related work are presented in Sect. 2, Sect. 3 establishes the need for a federated blockchain-integrated BPMS, and Sect. 4 describes the proposed architecture, while Sect. 5 illustrates its implementation. A comparative discussion of the federated and blockchain-centric approaches is presented in Sect. 6, followed by the conclusion of the paper.

2   Background and Related Work

The key advantages of blockchain, besides immutabiity, include: visibility (all authorised participants can view the transactions); validation (transactions are endorsed by peers through a designated consensus mechanism prior to being written to the chain); and resilience (a replicated ledger means there is no single point-of-failure).

A blockchain system can be *permissioned* (exercise membership control) or *permissionless* (publicly accessible). For example, Ethereum[1] [3] is (by default) a permissionless blockchain platform, where any peer can join to read or submit transactions at any time. Moreover, there is no central entity to manage membership, although private and permissioned blockchains can also be configured. Permissioned blockchain systems are designed to better address concerns around transaction security, privacy and scalability [1]. Hyperledger Fabric[2] [4] is an example of a permissioned blockchain framework. Another key aspect of blockchain technology is the provision of so-called *smart contracts* [5,15], i.e. executable scripts that reside on the blockchain and automate the steps and rules corresponding to the business logic of the bespoke transactional operations.

In recent research efforts towards integrating blockchain technology with BPM [6,10,19], the authors propose an architecture that tightly integrates business process execution with blockchain by encapsulating the entire business process logic into smart contracts. In this approach, a translator component takes a process specification as input and generates a set of corresponding smart contracts per process instance. In addition, a choreography monitor uses smart contracts to control a collaborative business process. A prototype has been developed for the Ethereum platform [19].

Architectural design issues of blockchain based systems with an eye towards quality and performance attributes are addressed in [20] in the form of a taxonomy and flowchart. Other performance issues that have been addressed are availability [18] and latency [21]. Methods for optimising execution of business processes on an Ethereum blockchain by improving data structures and runtime components are discussed in [6] and demonstrated in a prototype called Caterpillar [8]. Approaches for implementing collaborative, data-aware business processes on blockchain using the business artifact paradigm are discussed in [2,7], focussing on a new business collaboration language.

Sturm et al. [14] develop a generic approach to control-flow management within the blockchain by having one contract that handles choice and parallel structures. However, the control-flow capabilities are limited and data management is not discussed. There are also a plethora of approaches to inter-organisational process management that use platforms and environments other than blockchain, for example [9,11,13].

All these related approaches have helped to locate our work in context. However, our approach is different in that we believe that the essential functionality

---

[1] https://www.ethereum.org/.
[2] https://www.hyperledger.org/projects/fabric.

of a BPM system should not be migrated to the blockchain. Instead, we explore a lean approach (along the lines of [14]) wherein the BPM system can interface with the blockchain as a repository of reliable data and for executing key contractual terms through smart contracts.

3   Towards a Federated Blockchain-Integrated BPMS

Consider the pharmaceutical use case scenario shown in Fig. 1. In this crossorganisational process, a **Pharmacy** places an order for medical supplies with its **Distributor**, who in turn requests the production of the pharmaceuticals by the **Manufacturer**. Once the pharmaceuticals are manufactured, they are delivered to the Distributor who then sends them to the Pharmacy.

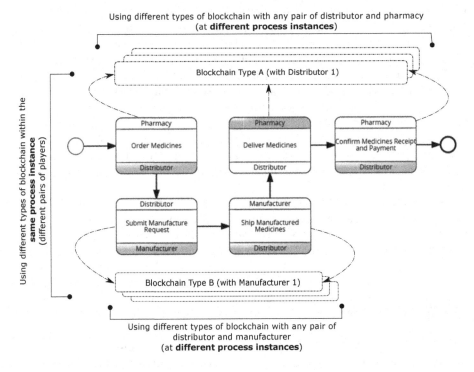

Fig. 1. Pharmaceutical supply process - multiple ledgers

When this process is executed, there is a potential for conflict across different parties. For example, if the Distributor fails to deliver the ordered pharmaceuticals on time, the Distributor may blame the Manufacturer for being late with production, or the Distributor may dispute the date and time when it received the original order. Therefore, the use of blockchain in recording the process transactions can be beneficial. Moreover, each organisation can exercise full control over their own private business process, and share information of only selected activities that involve cross-organisational interactions, as shown in Fig. 1.

There are many desirable features of this approach. Firstly, the parties in the process do not need to agree on a common inter-organisational process. They may even be on different blockchain platforms so long as they are compatible. Secondly, the lower transparency requirement will increase the willingness of the parties to cooperate with each other. Thirdly, there is more scalability in such an arrangement since in general a pharmacy will deal with multiple distributors, and a distributor, in turn, with multiple manufacturers. Thus, this use case calls for a more *flexible, decentralised, loosely-coupled* and *distributed* approach based on platform heterogeneity, for both two-party and multi-party interactions, which minimises the need for interactions with the blockchain platform.

Towards a Federated Approach. We propose a federated, blockchain integrated BPMS architecture to address the issues identified above. Such an architecture should provide the following properties:

- **Separation of Concerns:** A clear separation of capabilities should be maintained between business logic operations and distributed transactional execution records, with the aim of minimising the performance hit on blockchain operations and maximising the fit-for-purpose capabilities of the BPMS and blockchain platforms.
- **Platform Heterogeneity:** The architecture should allow the use of more than one compatible blockchain platform *within and across a composite set of interacting process instances.*
- **Compartmentalisation of Interactions:** A requirement that all interactions between any two participating parties need to be transparent to all parties involved should not be imposed. A blockchain-centric architecture may perhaps support this through the use of, for example, separate permissioned channels, but this should not be seen as a necessary realisation, and it still imposes the requirement that they share the same blockchain platform.
- **Single-party Interaction:** The architecture should not assume that all interactions between a business process and a blockchain involve multi-party communication. Hence, it should support simple single-party interaction between an organisation's business process and its corresponding blockchain.

4   Conceptual Architecture

In our federated approach, each organisation hosts a discrete BPMS that encapsulates a service or middleware component through which it will delegate designated tasks, designed to perform a required inter-organisational activity, within a process execution instance. The service will then interact with a properly configured blockchain network.

Each participating service in an inter-organisational process is granted authorisation to a discrete permissioned *channel* (or other authenticating, secure

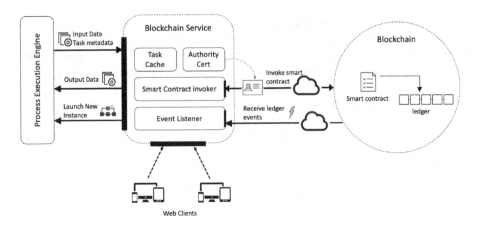

Fig. 2. Conceptual internal architecture

pipeline) on a blockchain network. A channel is a private overlay that partitions a blockchain network to provide data isolation and confidentiality [1]. Whenever a new block is written, an event notification is generated by the blockchain platform and then relayed to the BPMS through the service. The service will by default listen for events as they occur, but it may also be configured to periodically request the event history from past blocks, to accommodate those deployments where connection to the blockchain network is not always available. The service will take one of three actions for each received event notification, depending on how the service has been configured for each event: (1) release a task that has been waiting for the event to occur; (2) launch a new process instance, using the event as a trigger; or (3) ignore the event.

Hence, the only information exchanged between organisations is that required for work to be handed over and performed within each organisation (e.g. purchase order, invoice, contract, application). The state of a process instance can be inferred from the history of data associated with it on the blockchain, for example an order has been placed, a shipment was sent, a payment was made, etc. This eliminates the need for sharing additional information about exact process state on the blockchain, or any process definitions, business logic and rules, organisational data, or resource allocations that should remain private to their respective organisations.

A transaction (such as placing a purchase order) submitted by one organisation to the blockchain will, within a short period, be written to a block on the blockchain after it is validated by other peer nodes on the network using a validation algorithm, and ordered along with other transactions into a block structure. The creation of a new block will trigger an event notification which may be used by another organisation to complete a task in one of its own processes or to commence a new process instance (see Sect. 5 for more details).

An internal architecture of the proposed approach is given in Fig. 2. The BPMS of an organisation will delegate the execution of certain tasks to the blockchain service (middleware component) using the appropriate API along with the requisite data. The subcomponents of the middleware are:

- **Smart Contract Invoker:** Performs smart contract calls on the blockchain to either query the current instance data that has been written to the chain, or requests the creation of a new transaction to store data to be shared with another organisation.
- **Event Listener:** Listens and responds to events generated by the blockchain network each time a new transaction is created. An event may trigger the completion of a waiting task, or the launch of a new process instance via a call to the BPM engine's API.
- **Task Cache:** Stores tasks that are waiting for some event to occur on the blockchain, that is some specific data to be made available from another organisation (e.g. order received, invoice produced, etc). When the designated event occurs, that task can be further processed and/or completed, allowing its parent process instance to continue.
- **Authority Certificate Store:** Stores the private and public keys authorising the service to access the channel to read from and submit to the ledger on behalf of its owner organisation. Each call of a smart contract must be accompanied by the appropriate certificates.

5 Implementation

A prototype service that implements the conceptual architecture described in Sect. 4 has been realised in the YAWL business process management environment [16]. YAWL was selected because it is robust, fully open-source, and offers a service-oriented architecture, allowing an interactive blockchain service to be implemented independent of existing components. However, the generic federated architecture is not limited to the YAWL environment, but rather is applicable to any BPMS that supports the addition of service-oriented or middleware components for interacting with external networks and applications. Importantly, absolutely no changes were required to be made to the YAWL environment itself to enable support for communication and interaction with a blockchain network. The YAWL Blockchain Service, and its source code, can be freely downloaded from the YAWL repository[3].

For this prototype implementation, a Hyperledger Fabric blockchain network was chosen, because it is open-source, can be deployed freely, does not require crypto-currency payments for its operations and supports a permissioned network natively. Again, the architecture is not limited by this choice; other blockchain platforms may be used.

The Blockchain Service has been developed as a YAWL custom service and so may have tasks assigned to it at design time via the process editor. At runtime,

---

[3] https://github.com/yawlfoundation/yawl.

the engine delegates all such assigned tasks to the service for action, passing task input data and metadata to it via a specific process engine API. Communication between the YAWL Blockchain Service and the Hyperledger Fabric network is handled via the Java software development kit (SDK) for Hyperledger[4]. Each organisation maintains its own discrete YAWL environment and Blockchain Service.

5.1   Event Handling

The architecture leverages the event generating capabilities of the blockchain platform to provide change-of-state announcements in the end-to-end process, in particular notifying parties in cross-organisational processes of actions that have been taken by others. Events of interest can be used to release a task that has been waiting for an action to occur, or can signify the triggering of a new process instance within an organisation.

For a task that has been designated to wait for an action, a dedicated data structure, which specifies the event to wait for and the values that uniquely identify the event as related to the current end-to-end process instance, is included as an input parameter of the task. On being delegated the task at runtime, the Blockchain Service stores details of the task, and the specifics of the $WAIT$ data values, and compares each incoming event with those parameters. When a match occurs, the task is updated with the values attached to the event, and released, i.e. returned to the core BPMS engine, allowing the process instance to continue.

The other type of event of interest to the Blockchain Service signifies the triggering of a new case instance. For example, if a pharmacy raises a purchase order and submits it to a blockchain, the event produced by the blockchain when the order transaction is written to a block can be captured by the Blockchain Service of a pharmaceuticals distributor and used to trigger the creation of a new process to fulfil that order (see Sect. 5.2 below for more details). Events can be defined as process triggering events via a dynamically loaded configuration file, or via an input data variable for a task, or by using an administration tool.

5.2   Illustrative Example

An example execution of typical interactions among the three organisations in the supply chain scenario of Sect. 3 is illustrated in Fig. 3. The processes have been somewhat simplified for clarity in the discussion below, and are depicted in the YAWL language.

There are three interacting organisations: a *Pharmacy* that places orders for the supply of pharmaceuticals, a *Distributor* that fulfils those orders, and a *Manufacturer* that fabricates and supplies pharmaceuticals for distribution. The Pharmacy interacts only with the Distributor, similarly the Manufacturer interacts only with the Distributor, and consequently the Distributor interacts with both. To ensure data isolation and confidentiality, two channels

---

[4] https://github.com/hyperledger/fabric-sdk-java.

are created, one *Pharmacy* $\longleftrightarrow$ *Distributor* (called *chPharmDist*), the other *Manufacturer* $\longleftrightarrow$ *Distributor* (*chManuDist*). Importantly, all internal processes remains private to each organisation, only the transactional data necessary to collaborate with another organisation is shared via the blockchain.

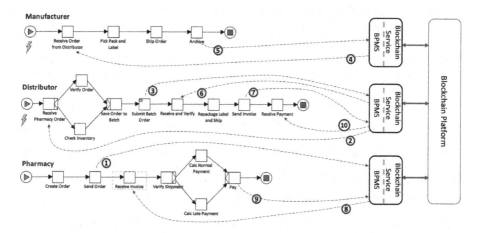

Fig. 3. Inter-organisational process interactions – supply chain example

While this scenario concerns a specific pharmacy-distributor-manufacturer, more generally a distributor would deal with a number of different pharmacies and manufacturers, and vice versa, all of which would potentially participate as peers within the blockchain platform and may play a role in the validation consensus that occurs when a transaction is submitted to the chain. Further, it is of course also possible to have a single channel for all three parties if desired.

To illustrate a complete sequence of interactions, with reference to Fig. 3 and the numeric labelling within it:

1. A composite process instance begins with the pharmacy process, when a new order is generated and then sent, i.e. submitted and subsequently written to a new block on the chain via a task delegated to its YAWL Blockchain Service.
2. Since the permissioned channel *chPharmDist* is shared by the Pharmacy and the Distributor, the Distributor's Blockchain Service detects the new *BlockEvent* and interprets it as a trigger to launch a new instance of its internal 'supply' process. The transaction data sent with the event (i.e. the purchase order) is used as the originating data for the new instance.
3. The Distributor adds the order to a batch, then at a designated time submits the batch order to the Manufacturer via submission to the blockchain via the shared *chManuDist* channel shared by those two organisations.
4. The Manufacturer's service receives the write *BlockEvent*, which triggers a new instance of its own 'manufacture' process, using the transaction data in the event (i.e. the batch order) as originating data.

5. Once the Manufacturer ships the order, the process archives the order details on the blockchain.
6. This *BlockEvent* triggers the release of the waiting *Receive and Verify* task in the Distributor's process, allowing that process to continue.
7. Later, an invoice is produced by the Distributor and submitted to the blockchain via the *chPharmDist* channel.
8. The subsequent writing of the invoice to the chain causes a *BlockEvent* that triggers the release of the waiting *Receive Invoice* task in the Pharmacy's process.
9. Eventually, the Pharmacy pays the invoice by submitting the payment transfer details to the chain.
10. The payment causes a *BlockEvent* that triggers the release of the waiting *Receive Payment* task in the Distributor's process.

Significantly, this example illustrates that secure inter-organisational process automation can be achieved using a federated architecture, and that the approach affords several concrete advantages when compared to the more heavyweight, blockchain-centric architectures:

– Efforts to combine the three processes into one overarching, monolithic, end-to-end process model are no longer required, negating the need for a great deal of collaboration between all parties, and the translation of the result into a set of factory smart contracts. The architecture also avoids the need for the creation, verification and storage of a new set of smart contracts for every instance of the inter-organisational process.
– Because all business logic, branching rules, resources allocations, etc. are handled by the BPMS, the smart contracts here are not overloaded with procedural code, resulting in much simpler, faster to process transactions. In this example, the smart contracts define data structures for order, invoice and payment, and a trivial invoke function that either submits a transaction or performs a query over existing blocks. The data structures are used to (de)serialise JSON strings passed to/from the BPMS into block data.
– There is no need to 'centralise' the process on the blockchain. Each organisation retains autonomy of its own processes, and the foci of operations are retained within the processes of each organisation's BPMS.
– There is no requirement for the creation and maintenance of the "intricate set of components" [19], prerequisite to the heavyweight architecture. Only a standard BPMS environment, a simple middleware service and vanilla blockchain network are needed.
– Unlike many blockchain-centric architectures, there is no requirement for a central 'mediator' process to choreograph the interactions between each organisation's processes.
– There are no limitations placed on the types of process patterns supported. Any pattern supported by the process language used by the process execution environment (i.e. the BPMS) can be used in this approach, including those more complex patterns that are difficult, if not impossible, to transform into

a smart contract, since all process executions are contained within the BPMS, rather than on the blockchain.

- An unimpeachable audit trail is stored on the blockchain(s) and can be extrapolated for all inter-process activity instances between organisation pairs.

6   Discussion and Conclusion

Many blockchain-centric approaches use a blockchain monolithically as an entire execution platform for business processes. Thus, a potentially large volume of data, including process definitions in the form of smart contracts, business rule definitions, datasets representing the work of a process instance, as well as its constantly updating state information, is written to, read from, and executed on the blockchain. Depending on the smart contracts and business rules executed, such data could contain potentially-confidential internal data of an organisation, thus inadvertently and unnecessarily exposing private data to external parties.

As per our case example (Fig. 3), it will require 20 large, custom contracts to be created (one for each task) in such blockchain-centric architectures versus 7 short, generic contracts that merely write important transactions to the blockchain in our approach. Additionally, each custom contract will require considerable effort for verification, and the blind trust of each organisation that the translation tool generates error-free smart contracts. Each update of a smart contract requires that each peer must compile, instantiate and validate it before it is committed to the blockchain, thus consuming resources and adding to the overhead of the blockchain's performance.

It is clear that blockchain is much more expensive as a medium for processing and storage than traditional media. Hence, it should be used as sparingly as possible by minimising both the size of smart contracts and the amount of data stored, while maintaining trust by means of a reliable audit trail. Extraneous processing and data should go to traditional platforms that offer better performance, flexibility and technology heterogeneity, and less visibility across parties. We are not convinced that it is necessary to reinvent the functionality of a BPM engine, which includes complex control flow management, data management and resource allocation, within a blockchain platform.

As we have demonstrated in our implementation, it is less work to integrate blockchain into an application with our federated approach, when compared to the more heavyweight blockchain-centric architectures. To fully transfer all the features of an industrial strength BPM system onto a blockchain platform could amount to a very long, risky and expensive undertaking, especially when considering the non-trivial processes in real-world scenarios. Our prototype illustrates the advantages of dedicating the existing capabilities of BPMS for process automation, and those of blockchain as an immutable, distributed ledger, to automate secure, cross-organisational process interactions without the overheads necessitated by the heavyweight, blockchain-centric approach.

We believe our proposal aligns better with the underlying philosophy of blockchain technology based on distributed autonomous organisations (DAOs)

[12]. We have presented a conceptual architecture and an implementation that demonstrates the feasibility of the approach. The comparisons presented here are mostly qualitative; a more thorough empirical comparison through experiments and quantitative data is needed and it will form our future work. More work is also needed to optimise the distribution of on-chain and off-chain data, and to validate the applicability of the federated approach with different types of scenarios and use cases.

References

1. Androulaki, E., Barger, A., Bortnikov, V., Cachin, C., et al.: Hyperledger Fabric: a distributed operating system for permissioned blockchains. In: Proceedings of the Thirteenth EuroSys Conference, p. 30. ACM (2018)
2. Astigarraga, T., et al.: Empowering business-level blockchain users with a rules framework for smart contracts. In: Pahl, C., Vukovic, M., Yin, J., Yu, Q. (eds.) ICSOC 2018. LNCS, vol. 11236, pp. 111–128. Springer, Cham (2018). https://doi.org/10.1007/978-3-030-03596-9_8
3. Buterin, V.: Ethereum: a next-generation smart contract and decentralized application platform (2014). https://github.com/ethereum/wiki/wiki/White-Paper
4. Cachin, C.: Architecture of the hyperledger blockchain fabric. In: Distributed Cryptocurrencies and Consensus Ledgers, vol. 310, p. 4 (2016)
5. Christidis, K., Devetsikiotis, M.: Blockchains and smart contracts for the internet of things. IEEE Access 4, 2292–2303 (2016)
6. García-Bañuelos, L., Ponomarev, A., Dumas, M., Weber, I.: Optimized execution of business processes on blockchain. In: Carmona, J., Engels, G., Kumar, A. (eds.) BPM 2017. LNCS, vol. 10445, pp. 130–146. Springer, Cham (2017). https://doi.org/10.1007/978-3-319-65000-5_8
7. Hull, R., Batra, V.S., Chen, Y.-M., Deutsch, A., Heath III, F.F.T., Vianu, V.: Towards a shared ledger business collaboration language based on data-aware processes. In: Sheng, Q.Z., Stroulia, E., Tata, S., Bhiri, S. (eds.) ICSOC 2016. LNCS, vol. 9936, pp. 18–36. Springer, Cham (2016). https://doi.org/10.1007/978-3-319-46295-0_2
8. López-Pintado, O., García-Bañuelos, L., Dumas, M., Weber, I., Ponomarev, A.: Caterpillar: a business process execution engine on the ethereum blockchain. Softw. Pract. Exp. 49(7), 1162–1193 (2019)
9. Mendling, J., Hafner, M.: From inter-organizational workflows to process execution: generating BPEL from WS-CDL. In: Meersman, R., Tari, Z., Herrero, P. (eds.) OTM 2005. LNCS, vol. 3762, pp. 506–515. Springer, Heidelberg (2005). https://doi.org/10.1007/11575863_70
10. Mendling, J., Weber, I., van der Aalst, W., vom Brocke, J., et al.: Blockchains for business process management - challenges and opportunities. ACM Trans. Manag. Inf. Syst. 9(1), 41–416 (2018)
11. Narendra, N.C., Norta, A., Mahunnah, M., Ma, L., Maggi, F.M.: Sound conflict management and resolution for virtual-enterprise collaborations. Serv. Oriented Comput. Appl. 10(3), 233–251 (2015). https://doi.org/10.1007/s11761-015-0183-0
12. Norta, A.: Creation of smart-contracting collaborations for decentralized autonomous organizations. In: Matulevičius, R., Dumas, M. (eds.) BIR 2015. LNBIP, vol. 229, pp. 3–17. Springer, Cham (2015). https://doi.org/10.1007/978-3-319-21915-8_1

13. Norta, A., Grefen, P., Narendra, N.C.: A reference architecture for managing dynamic inter-organizational business processes. Data Knowl. Eng. **91**, 52–89 (2014)
14. Sturm, C., Szalanczi, J., Schönig, S., Jablonski, S.: A lean architecture for blockchain based decentralized process execution. In: Daniel, F., Sheng, Q.Z., Motahari, H. (eds.) BPM 2018. LNBIP, vol. 342, pp. 361–373. Springer, Cham (2019). https://doi.org/10.1007/978-3-030-11641-5_29
15. Szabo, N.: Formalizing and securing relationships on public networks. First Monday **2**(9) (1997)
16. ter Hofstede, A., van der Aalst, W., Adams, M., Russell, N. (eds.): Modern Business Process Automation: YAWL and Its Support Environment. Springer, Heidelberg (2010). https://doi.org/10.1007/978-3-642-03121-2
17. Underwood, S.: Blockchain beyond bitcoin. Commun. ACM **59**(11), 15–17 (2016)
18. Weber, I., Gramoli, V., Ponomarev, A., Staples, M., et al.: On availability for blockchain-based systems. In: 2017 IEEE 36th Symposium on Reliable Distributed Systems (SRDS), pp. 64–73 (2017)
19. Weber, I., Xu, X., Riveret, R., Governatori, G., Ponomarev, A., Mendling, J.: Untrusted business process monitoring and execution using blockchain. In: La Rosa, M., Loos, P., Pastor, O. (eds.) BPM 2016. LNCS, vol. 9850, pp. 329–347. Springer, Cham (2016). https://doi.org/10.1007/978-3-319-45348-4_19
20. Xu, X., Weber, I., Staples, M., Zhu, L., et al.: A taxonomy of blockchain-based systems for architecture design. In: ICSA, pp. 243–252. IEEE (2017)
21. Yasaweerasinghelage, R., Staples, M., Weber, I.: Predicting latency of blockchain-based systems using architectural modelling and simulation. In: ICSA, pp. 253–256. IEEE (2017)

PROCLAIM: An Unsupervised Approach to Discover Domain-Specific Attribute Matchings from Heterogeneous Sources

Molood Arman[1,2]([⊠]) [ID], Sylvain Wlodarczyk[1] [ID],
Nacéra Bennacer Seghouani[2] [ID], and Francesca Bugiotti[2] [ID]

[1] Services Pétroliers Schlumberger, 34000 Montpellier, France
{marman2,swlodarczyk}@slb.com
[2] Université Paris-Saclay, CNRS, Laboratoire de Recherche en Informatique,
91405 Orsay, France
{nacera.seghouani,francesca.bugiotti}@lri.fr

Abstract. Schema matching is a critical problem in many applications where the main goal is to match attributes coming from heterogeneous sources. In this paper, we propose PROCLAIM (PROfile-based Cluster-Labeling for AttrIbute Matching), an automatic, unsupervised clustering-based approach to match attributes of a large number of heterogeneous sources. We define the concept of attribute profile to characterize the main properties of an attribute using: (i) the statistical distribution and the dimension of the attribute's values, (ii) the name and textual descriptions related to the attribute. The attribute matchings produced by PROCLAIM give the best representation of heterogeneous sources thanks to the cluster-labeling function we defined. We evaluate PROCLAIM on 45,000 different data sources coming from oil and gas authority open data website (The data is published under Creative Commons Attribution-NonCommercial-ShareAlike 4.0 International (CC BY-NC-SA 4.0)). The results we obtain are promising and validate our approach.

1 Introduction

During the last years, the availability of multiple and heterogeneous data sources has given new perspectives to the schema matching problem which is a fundamental step for data integration. A large number of research works exist in the literature, the main task in these approaches is to identify the correlation between the attributes using dataset values, semantic and syntactic rules to detect the correspondence between attributes during the schema matching process [1]. Most of the works on schema integration assumed a global (mediated) schema and then tried to find a solution for better matching on mostly a pairwise matching between the source schema and the mediated schema. In this context it is very difficult to define a global schema that matches all the attributes of a given domain [10]. Moreover, real world data is always noisy and for most of integration methods, data cleaning is needed. However, in terms of big data,

N. Herbaut and M. La Rosa (Eds.): CAiSE Forum 2020, LNBIP 386, pp. 14–28, 2020.
https://doi.org/10.1007/978-3-030-58135-0_2

data cleaning is expensive and time consuming. In this paper, we develop an heuristic method which can deal with real world and massive data.

In this paper, we present PROCLAIM (PROfile-based Cluster-Labeling for AttrIbute Matching), an unsupervised method for matching attributes coming from a large number and heterogeneous sources in a specific domain. Our results show that PROCLAIM is an effective fully automatic method to discover a set of meaningful vocabularies which are the backbone of the definition of a specific domain. PROCLAIM defines the concept of attribute profile by taking into account the data type using: (i) the statistical distribution and the dimension of the attribute's values, and (ii) the name and textual descriptions of the attribute. These properties give a unified representation to each attribute. The cluster-labeling function takes as input these properties to automatically assign a set of labels to a high number of attributes.

The paper is organized as follows: Sect. 2 reviews the related studies on schema matching and the available tools. Section 3 presents a brief overview of PROCLAIM. Sections 4, 5 and 6 detail each building block of PROCLAIM. Section 7 illustrates the results of our experiments in two different domains. Finally, Sect. 8 draws some future steps.

2   Related Work

Knowledge Base (KB) construction is a recurrent problem in industry and research and includes problems of data extraction, cleaning, and integration [6]. A significant amount of work has been done in recent years for automatic construction of knowledge bases. However, the first step of KB construction, which is defining a global schema with the aim of populating the KB, still requires a manual effort [15]. Several previous researches were mainly focused on extracting data from unstructured data such as texts. Open Information Extraction systems are not concerned with the integration of extracted entities and their properties from different sources with unified names. Because of this limitation the resulting knowledge bases may the same entity represented multiple times with different names [15]. Other techniques, such as Biperpedia [9], use search engine query logs in addition to text to discover attributes. This process involves numerous trained classifiers and corresponding labeled training data. Most of the automatic KB construction systems were focused on retrieving facts and entities from unstructured datasets. To our knowledge, integrating the existing structured sources in the knowledge bases has not been considered in the process of constructing the KB automatically.

A large number of publications focused only on schema matching. In this context, schema matching identifies the correspondences between similar elements belonging to different schemas. IntelliLIGHT [8] is a system looking in large-scale structured data sets which aims to locate and retrieve needed data in a specific domain. It proposes a method which ranks the main data tables taking as output the ones having a higher score. PROCLAIM is a very different approach to the problem; instead of ranking the best available schema among different data sources, it provides a unified standard schema from all sources and generates a global schema for a domain automatically. UFO [11] is a data structure expressing various representations of the same concept as a data object and is capable of recognizing and mapping such objects in different data sources automatically. The WebTable system [3] is a search engine that ranks tables scraped from the web. In this approach, AcsDB is introduced as a database which contains a corpus of statistics on schema elements that is used to compute the probability of an attribute (the number of schemas containing the attribute divided by the total number of schemas) and the probability of an attribute conditioned on another attribute. WebTable autocompletes a schema (suggest additional related attributes for a given set of attributes) by using the probability of pair attributes in different schema to provide additional synonyms. In contrast, PROCLAIM focuses on all characteristics of all attributes to find the similar attributes in the provided schemas. The main goal of PROCLAIM is discovering the most complete global schema over the existing schemas in a domain.

3   PROCLAIM Overview

Schema matching aims at discovering semantic correspondences of attributes of schemas across heterogeneous sources. Our goal is to get a global attribute schema for all the independently developed schemas of the same domain which can be formalized as follows.

Given a set of schemas $S = \{S_1, S_2, ..., S_n\}$ and the set of all attributes $\mathcal{A}=\{A_1, A_2, ..., A_n\}$ belonging to these schemas, each A_i contains the whole set of attributes $(a_1, ..., a_m)$ used in the schema S_i. Let us consider a single *schema* (S) and its set of attributes (A) $(a_i \in A$ where $i \in [1:m])$. *Schema matching* selects sets of n-ary *mapping attributes* which together define similar groups of attributes (G_i), as illustrated in Example 1. All attributes are trivially a group by themselves. A *label (l)* can identify in the best way the essence of a semantic group of attributes. A *labeling function* $f_L(G)$ indicates the required process to define the label $(f_L : G \to L)$, where L is a set of labels $(l_i \in L; 0 \le i \le m)$ and G is a set of similar groups of attributes $(G_i \in G)$. The set of labels (L) identifies the elements of a global schema for the given set of schemas (**S**), this resulting schema is also the mediated or target schema.

Example 1. Consider three schemas as set of attributes about about rental cars descriptions:
$S_1 = \{$Fuel_Type, Location, Mileage, Name, Price, Year, Transmission$\}$
$S_2 = \{$Country, Disp., HP, Mileage, Price, Type$\}$
$S_3 = \{$fuel_type, maker, manufacture_year, mileage, model, price_eur, transmission$\}$
Also, consider the following attribute matches among the schemas:
$G_1 = \{$Fuel_Type, fuel_type, fuel, fuelType$\}$
$G_2 = \{$Location, Country, city, county_name, state_name$\}$
$G_3 = \{$Name, maker, brand$\}$

Consider these labels {Location, Brand, Fuel, ldots} extracted from the data sets. These labels will be assigned to each group of attribute (i.e. as follows: l_1 = $Fuel$, l_2 = $Location$, l_3 = $Brand$) and will define the names of the attributes of the global schema for a specific domain: L = {Fuel, Location, Brand, ... }.

The main question addressed in this research is how to define an automatic process that discovers a set of labels which can effectively represent a global attribute schema for a specific domain. The PROCLAIM method is proposed as an answer to this question. PROCLAIM is a new approach which enables the automatic holistic schema matching which leads to construction of a global attribute schema for a specific domain. Let us illustrate the procedure, by following the main steps it involves, with the help of Fig. 1:

1. a set of heterogeneous sources with different schema ($\mathbf{S}$) is provided as input;
2. the data from all sources are stored in columnar format storage;
3. the data type of each attribute is identified and data with the same data type are stored in the same set ($\mathbf{S}_{d_K}$);
4. an attribute profile is computed based on the specificity of each data type ($\mathbf{S}_{d_K}$). This profile for all kinds of attributes can contain at most four properties (statistics, description, unit, and name property). Then each profile of attributes can contain at most four properties. The assigned profile to each attribute will be converted to a numerical vector;
5. an automatic labelling process is defined to find all similar attributes and gives a unified name to each of them. This process includes two principal components: (1) finding the most similar attributes from different schemas, (2) giving an automatic label to each attribute by a defined labeling function (L_f). A density based clustering algorithm will be applied on the numerical profiles for finding the most similar attributes. Each profile vector represents a unique attribute;
6. the list of automatically computed labels will define a global attribute schema for a specific domain.

As explained in detail in the following sections, PROCLAIM can be applied on real-life noisy data. The method is designed to handle a large number of heterogeneous schemas and proposes a unified numerical profiling of information of any data type. The approach enables the usage of common machine learning algorithms such as clustering. Finally the automatic labeling and merging of clusters allow the definition of a global schema that represents the synthesis of the heterogeneous schemas.

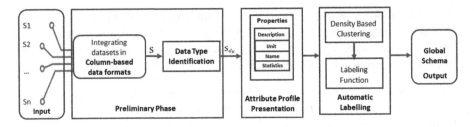

Fig. 1. The framework of PROCLAIM to discover a global schema

4   Preliminary Phase

Some of the building blocks of PROCLAIM can be considered as initial steps to prepare the original datasets. Two main steps are defined as the initial steps in the preliminary phase of PROCLAIM (1) targeting data into a columnar datastore, (2) identifying the data type.

4.1   Column-Based Data Formats

Column-based data formats organize data in a set of tables. Each table contains a set of rows, and each row has a set of columns, each with a name and a value. Rows in a table are not required to have the same attributes. Data access operations are usually over individual rows and show the best performances when retrieve only a subset of the attributes of a table, when data sets are sparse and contain lots of empty values [12]. Moreover column-based data formats process big datasets efficiently since provide large-scale parallelization and effective partitioning strategies. PROCLAIM for its calculation needs a tuple for each value of attributes showing the name of the attribute and its value. In this case, storing the data in columnar-based format is much efficient.

4.2   Data Type Identification

When the search space is large (the number of attributes or schemas are big), matching the complete input of schemas may require long execution times, and achieving high quality results may be difficult. One way to reduce the search space is to find the similar attributes within the same data types. The heterogeneous sources provide attributes in different data types. Since the type of the attributes may not be provided in the metadata of sources, we need to identify the types given the values. One main problem in this step is the fact that the original datasets are not clean. We have to consider the type based on the data type of the majority of the instances (values). Here, we just consider five data types but this set can be extended if it is necessary:

– NUMERICAL representing all attributes which its value just contain integer or float.

- CATEGORICAL containing all strings, characters and mix data type.
- DATE representing date and time such as datetime, timestamps and etc.
- RARE classifying attributes which they have less than 10 instances.
- UNIQUE referring to attributes with unique value (cardinality is equal to 1).

Formally, let d_k be the data type of an attribute a_i with probability $p \geq$ *threshold* (e.g. *threshold* = 0.8) where $a_i \in \mathcal{A}$ and $d_k \in \{$ NUMERICAL, CATEGORICAL, DATE, RARE, UNIQUE$\}$ where k $\in$ [1,5]. *Data Type function* (F_D) $(F_D : \mathcal{A} \rightarrow \{$ NUMERICAL, CATEGORICAL, DATE, RARE, UNIQUE$\}$; $F_D(a_i) = d_K)$ pre-classified the attributes of the whole dataset into maximum five categories $(\mathbf{S}_{d_K})$ which contain attributes with the same data type.

5 Attribute Profile Representation

Once we have all the attributes belonging to the same data type $(\mathbf{S}_g)$ we can group them to discover attributes coming from different schemas which contain the same information (e.g., {name, maker, brand} in our example). PROCLAIM performs clustering and labeling based on the computation of a similarity matrix of numerical profiles of attributes. Before applying our algorithm, we must convert an attribute to a numerical profile based on its data type. According to our representation any attribute is characterized by a maximum of four components according to the data type to which it belongs. These components are description, unit, name, and statistics. In this section we provide a description of each component of the profile and its contribution in the analysis of the attributes classified in any of the six data types introduced in the previous section. Notice that the RARE type attributes are ignored due to the impossibility to compute a valid statistic.

Description Property. The majority of datasets have a descriptive part for the schema where the meaning of each attribute can be found. In other cases, the description is not provided but the used values belong to domain specific terms or abbreviations and this description can be retrieved, for example, using domain specific Wikis.

To create the description profile, first of all, we remove the stop-words and then we apply the stemming method over a bag of tokens. Then for each description, the stems and the occurrence of each term (in all the different descriptions for any specified attribute) is used to build the description profiles. Removing stop-words in a specific domain is necessary, since these words can appear in almost all descriptions and can cause false similarities (e.g., for the domain of cars, the words such as car, vehicle, automobile and etc, are the domain stop-words). We then transform the descriptions to categorical variables. Next, feature engineering is required to encode the different categories into a suitable numerical feature vector. One-hot encoding is a simple but efficient widely-used encoding method [4]. An example of converting categorical variables for some attributes to numerical values can be seen in Table 1.

Table 1. One-hot encoding for converting descriptions to numerical feature

Attribute	displac	volum	engin	cc	repres	kw	ccm
ENGINE_DISPLACEMENT	0	0	0	0	0	0	1
ENGINE_POWER	0	0	0	0	0	1	0
DISP.	1	0	1	0	1	0	0
ENGINE	1	1	1	1	0	0	0

Unit Property. Dimensions and units are fundamental tools to explain the characterization of phenomena [13]. A dimension is a measure of a physical variable by fundamental quantities without numerical value, such as distance, time, mass, and temperature. However, a unit is a specific way to assign a measurement (with numerical value) to the dimension, e.g., a dimension is length, whereas meters or feet are relative units that describes length [13]. Dimensions and units are commonly confused, despite the fact that the solution to most problems must include units. The distribution of the same entity in different units can be shifted, but by consideration of the same dimension, the similarity of shifted distribution can be found. Also, attributes with units related to same dimension are related to each other through a conversion factor, such as Kelvin or Celsius which measures the dimension of temperature and they can convert to each other. Given a dataset, the related units can be found thanks to the descriptive part of the schema or taking into account also the instances (near the value or in a separated column). The units and their mapped dimensions of attributes can be extracted and recorded separately. In Table 2 we show dimensions and units characterizing some attributes of our running example. The dimension is also encoded using one-hot encoding approach.

Table 2. Some attributes with their units and associated dimension

Attribute	Unit	Dimension
ENGINE_DISPLACEMENT	CCM	VOLUME
ENGINE_POWER	KW	POWER
PRICE_EUR	EUR	PRICE
ENGINE	CC	VOLUME

Name Property. The name of an attribute can also be useful for the analysis. Names often contain concatenated words and abbreviations. Thus, they first need to be normalized before they are used to construct a profile to compute linguistic similarities. First tokenization is applied but it may not be enough; e.g for the name 'vehicleType', the name should be split into word 'vehicle' and 'Type'. In this regard, we compare all names of other attributes and see if one of them is part of the name string, this breakdown will be done.

Statistics Property. The statistics profiles concern CATEGORICAL and NUMER-
ICAL data types. PROCLAIM uses descriptive statistical analysis to produce a
profile for each attribute which not only defines the characteristics of an attribute
but also enables comparing the profiles to find similarities. In the following, we
list the most important statistical measurements regarding NUMERICAL and CAT-
EGORICAL data types.

- NUMERICAL data type:
  For the NUMERICAL data type, there are several measures that can be
  studied. The domain under analysis and the characteristics of analyzed
  data will help us to select the significant ones. These measures can be vari-
  ability or dispersion of distribution of values per each attribute, symmetry
  of the distribution, the number of instances (cardinality) and central ten-
  dency.
- CATEGORICAL data type
  For the CATEGORICAL data type, the considered statistics profile contains
  the top most frequent values among all instances of one attribute. This
  set of top most frequent instances can design a pattern for an attribute.

Since other components of attribute profiles are encoded using one-hot encoding
approach we decided to apply the same method to the statistics profile. First log
transform will normalize the distribution with left or right skewness, then the
distribution is presented into categorical scale using binning and finally encoded.
We obviously lose the numerical nature of the statistics but we can merge easily
this vector with the other vectors without a normalization issue.

Table 3. Statistics profile

Attribute	5%	25%	50%	75%	95%	Count
DISP.	90.9	113.75	144.5	180.0	302.0	32
ENGINE	993.0	1198.00	1497.0	1995.0	2982.0	101
ENGINE_DISPLACEMENT	1124.0	1400.00	1600.0	1968.0	2967.0	158
ENGINE_POWER	44.0	65.00	80.0	103.0	161.5	114

Table 4. Normalized statistics profile

Attribute	5%	25%	50%	75%	95%	Count
DISP.	5	5	5	5	6	3
ENGINE	7	7	7	8	8	5
ENGINE_DISPLACEMENT	7	7	7	8	8	5
ENGINE_POWER	4	4	4	5	5	5

Example 2. In Table 3 we present the statistics profile for four numerical attributes. As a result of this analysis, we can see that the 'Engine' and 'Engine Displacement' have the same normalized distribution. Normalized data with log transformation is shown in Table 4.

For each attribute of the dataset, we compute the global profile which is made of four properties we described in this section. Each profile is built by considering the type of attribute and the global profile is finally converted into a numerical vector.

We finally produce a dataset that is made of a collection of vectors that will be the input for the next steps of the computation.

For each of the four properties, we propose a weighting factor on the properties that is adjusted according to the data type of the attribute. For example, for numerical and categorical variables, the attribute name can be ignored because this information is uncertain and the distribution of the values is very important.

6   Attribute Labeling

The attribute labeling is a three step process that (1) performs attribute clustering, (2) assigns a label to each cluster, and (3) merges clusters having the same label. Step 3 creates each single attribute of the global schema. In this section, we are going to detail each step of the process.

6.1   Clustering

The calibrated numerical vectors produced as described in Sect. 5 allow us to apply clustering to find similar groups of attributes ($G_i \in G$). PROCLAIM uses a density-based clustering method. Density-based clusters are connected, dense areas in the data space separated from each other by low density areas. Density-based clustering can be considered as a non-parametric approach, since this method makes no assumptions about the number of clusters or their distribution [5]. In higher-dimensional space the assumption of a certain number of clusters of a given distribution is very strong and may often be violated. However, other parameters should be identified, e.g., a density threshold that is the minimum number of points (MinPts) and the radius of a neighborhood (ϵ) in the case of DBSCAN [7] and OPTICS [2]. Sparse areas as opposed to high density areas are considered as outliers (noise). This results in having points in the sparse areas that are not assigned to any cluster since in general each outlier can be considered as one cluster containing just one element. As a result, 1) It is not necessary to specify the number of clusters; 2) It is not necessary that all the points belong to at least one cluster.

OPTICS [2] (Ordering PoinTs to Identify the Clustering Structure) and the aforementioned DBSCAN are two popular density based clustering algorithms. Despite all the similarities in the core concept of both algorithms, they have fundamental differences [2]. PROCLAIM uses OPTICS. In PROCLAIM, we want to reduce the chain of core profile effect [2] in order to have small clusters with very similar profiles; hence, we set a very small value (e.g. 3) for the MinPts input of OPTICS. We will then compute many clusters and have many outliers. To reduce the number of outliers we run OPTICS, a second time, again with a small value for the MinPts parameter only on the profiles that were considered as outliers. The clusters computed during the second step will be added to the clusters computed at the first step. With these two iterations, we increase the number of clusters and reduce the outliers.

6.2   Labeling Function

The labels for each cluster will be created by using the descriptions and names of all elements in each cluster. The stop words will be removed using the common linguistic stop words and the domain specific ones. The idea is to select the most frequent words, bigram, and trigram terms appearing in the description and name of each attribute of the cluster. Then, the most frequent term will be the label of the cluster as shown in Example 3.

Example 3. Consider $C_1 = \{ENGINE, DISP.\}$ as a cluster computed using the two-steps OPTICS algorithm. The descriptions gathered per each attribute are:

$Descr\_Engine$ = 'The displacement volume of the engine in CC.'
$Descr\_Disp.$ = ': Represents the engine displacement of the car'

The name profile of attributes can also be added to the descriptions: $Descr\_names = \{engine, disp\}$.

Furthermore, after removing the stop words, the following bag of words for each description will be generated:

$BOW\_Engine = \{$displacement$: 1,$ volume$: 1,$ engine$: 1,$ cc$: 1\}$
$BOW\_Disp. = \{$represents$: 1,$ engine$: 1,$ displacement$: 1,$ car$: 1\}$
$BOW\_names. = \{$engine$: 1,$ disp$: 1\}$

Moreover, we create a holistic bag of words by merging all the terms together associated with their total number of occurrences as follows:

$BOW\_total = \{$engine$: 3,$ displacement$: 2,$ volume$: 1,$ cc$: 1,$ represents$: 1\}$

By selecting the most represented term, we may produce some meaningless labels such as "displacement engine" rather than "engine displacement". To tackle this problem, we need to create a domain specific corpus and extract from it the bigrams and trigrams associated with the respective number of occurrences. This will be used to adjust and validate the labels.

Consider a created corpus in the cars domain which includes resources of glossaries, dictionaries, wikis and etc. which can easily be gathered online[1]. Now, all combinations of the highest frequency words from BOW_total will be considered to create the bigrams and trigrams which already exist in this domain (the meaningful N-grams) with respect to terms frequency in the corpus. The bigrams and trigrams selected will create a valid bag of terms. We will also add the most frequent word appearing in the corpus to this valid bag of terms. From Example 3

---

[1] Data from: https://www.kaggle.com/.

we have: Bag_of_terms = {engine displacement : 2, displacement volume : 1, engine : 3}. To get the selected label, we take from the bag of terms the term with the maximum number of occurrences with the priority first to the trigrams then bigrams and finally words.

The selected label for the cluster C_1 = {$ENGINE, DISP.$} is **engine displacement** even if the number of occurrences of **engine** is higher.

After labeling each cluster we can finally merge the clusters with the same label or labels that are synonyms (Example 4).

Example 4. Consider C_2 = {$ENGINE\_DISPLACEMENT, ENGINE\_POWER$} as another cluster computed using the two-step OPTICS algorithm. The bag of words retrieved from related descriptions for these attributes are:
$BOW\_Engine\_Displacement$ = {ccm : 1}
BOW_Engine_Power = {kw : 1}
BOW_names = {engine : 2, displacement : 1, power : 1}
As final result the output is:
Bag_of_terms = {engine displacement : 2, engine power : 1, engine : 3}

The computed label is again **engine displacement** which means that this cluster can be merged with cluster C_1 of the Example 3. Then the new cluster contains the following attribute {ENGINE, DISP., ENGINE_DISPLACEMENT, ENGINE_POWER}.

All the merged and labelled clusters generate a global schema for a specific domain. The label of different clusters in different data types can be the same which enables us to integrate the attributes together even if their data types were assigned wrongly in Sect. 4.2. PROCLAIM helps to integrate the data from different sources and also creates a general schema which can help for integration or new sources or to populate a knowledge base in the specific domain.

7   Experiment Results

In this section, we provide the experimental results on two datasets: one of them is our ongoing cars example and the second is from the oil and gas domain. The code of the experiment is implemented in Python 3.6.7. Parquet [14], a columnar datastore is used to store original datasets. Parquet is a free and open-source optimized column-oriented data storage developed on the Apache Hadoop ecosystem. To the best of our knowledge, there are no benchmark labeled datasets for comparing our results with another method. Therefore, for the car example, we have collected data from Kaggle challenges. For the Oil and Gas example, we use a large dataset.

Table 5. Car_Kaggle data set information as the input for PROCLAIM

Data set	Kaggle challenge name	#Attributes	#Descriptions	#Units	#Source records
S_1	Used cars price prediction	13	11	4	1000
S_2	Cars data	8	7	0	600
S_3	Personal cars classified	16	11	4	1000
S_4	Craigslist cars EDA	26	24	0	1000
S_5	Used cars database	20	12	1	1000
Sum	Car_Kaggle	70	65	9	4600

Car_Kaggle. The Car_Kaggle dataset was gathered from five different sources $(S_1,\ldots, S_5)$ about cars from different Kaggle challenges (see Footnote 1). The global Car_Kaggle dataset, after merging different sources contain 78 original attributes: 70 of them have different names; 65 out of 70 attributes contain descriptions and just 9 out of 70 attributes have the provided unit. In Table 5, we provide the details of each schema. As first step, we run data type identification in order to discover the type of each attribute. Data for this dataset can be split in four different types and, as we can see the RARE data type is not present. Unique attributes are discarded (6 attributes) and we compute the profile for the 64 remaining attributes (25 NUMERICAL, 35 CATEGORICAL and 4 DATE attributes) and automatically assign label to each attribute. To be able to evaluate PROCLAIM, we manually labeled all the attributes. A subset of PRO-CLAIM labels and manual labels can be seen in Table 2. To evaluate the quality of PROCLAIM labels, we used three metrics: *precision, recall* and *F-measure*. Precision is defined as the percentage of the correct labels. We compared manual labels with PROCLAIM labels. If the pair (PROCLAIM LABEL, MANUALLY ANNOTATED LABEL) matches, the label is considered as valid, as it can be seen in Table 6. Recall is the ratio of attributes with correct labels to all attributes (with or without labels). F-measure which is the harmonic mean of the precision and recall. This result is shown in Table 7. These measures were calculated separately for each set of attributes (of each data type) and finally for the whole set of attributes. As it can be seen in Table 7, precision is showing a good quality of labels but since the number of attributes and sources are not big, we expected not very high recall, but still this recall is promising for the schema matching problem which in this research is not the main concern. The main goal is to have the labels with high quality.

Table 6. Labeling for Car_Kaggle

Attributes	PROCLAIM labels	Annotated labels	Match
PRICE_EUR	Price converted	Price	1
PRICE	Price converted	Price	1
POWERPS	Power	Power	1
HP	Power	Power	1
WEIGHT	Weight	Weight	1
POSTALCODE	Weight	Address	0

Table 7. PROCLAIM evaluation

Data type	Precision	Recall	F-measure
NUMERICAL	85.7	85.7	85.7
CATEGORICAL	73.0	58.8	64.2
DATE	100	100	1
Overall	82.5	72.7	77.3

Oil_NorthSea Dataset. The North Sea Oil and Gas (Oil_NorthSea) dataset were gathered from OGA[2] (The Oil and Gas Authority Open Data) website which contains 43997 different sources with a total of 5260 attributes. 4713 of them have different names. The description is available for 3481 attributes and unit is provided for 1668 over 4713 attributes. We apply the same approach as described in Sect. 7. The number of different identified types of attributes is: 638 NUMERICAL, 631 CATEGORICAL, 46 DATE, 574 RARE and 2824 UNIQUE attributes. Since the number of attributes is too big to be entirely manually annotated, we asked domain experts to label random set of attributes (20 labels for NUMERICAL and CATEGORICAL attributes and all labels for DATE attributes - the number of DATE attributes are less than 50). We cannot calculate recall and f-measure here, since the manual labels are just provided for a subset of random labels. However, precision is calculated for these subsets for different experiments. Experiments are done for different profiles for each group of same data type attributes and the result is shown in Table 8. Cover data ratio measures the percentage of labeled attributes. The Covered_data ratio is showing a high percentage of considered attributes to discover the global schema. As can be

Table 8. Experiments results for different profiles subset

Data type	Profile	#Unlabeled Attr.	#Labeled Attr.	#Labels	Precision (%)	Covered_data (%)
Numerical	Stat.	84	554	107	58.1	86.8
	Descr.	122	516	112	93.25	80.9
	[Stat., Descr.]	53	585	128	86.4	91.6
	[Stat., Descr., Unit]	60	578	110	90.1	90.5
Categorical	Stat.	135	496	102	70.5	78.6
	Descr.	203	428	100	94.9	67.8
	[Stat., Descr.]	129	502	126	86.2	79.5
	[Stat., Descr., Unit]	121	510	130	92.1	80.8
Date	Descr.	16	30	3	100	65.2
	[Descr., Name]	5	41	7	94.3	89.1
	[Descr., Unit, Name[a]]	5	41	7	94.3	89.1
Total	[full profile]	186	1129	247	92.2	85.9

[a] Unit is not available for Date attributes

[2] The data is published under Creative Commons Attribution-NonCommercial-ShareAlike 4.0 International (CC BY-NC-SA 4.0).

seen, the precision of clusters for NUMERICAL, CATEGORICAL, and DATE data type is over 90% which is a promising result. The global schema created from the Oil_NorthSea dataset contains 247 labeled attributes which covers 86% of the 1315 original attributes belong to the NUMERICAL, CATEGORICAL, and DATE data types.

8   Conclusion and Future Works

Compared to the huge work on pairwise schema matching, research on holistic schema matching for more than two sources is still at an early stage. PROCLAIM is an efficient and effective way for schema matching and provides a consistent domain-specific attribute schema. Experiments show that thanks to our approach we can gather automatically more than 80% of vocabularies related to a domain and populate the knowledge bases with corresponding attributes from heterogeneous sources. In future work, our approach can be extended for handling new attributes from new sources and for enriching the set of labels by adding similar words from different thesauri and dictionaries.

References

1. Alwan, A.A., Nordin, A., Alzeber, M., Abualkishik, A.Z.: A survey of schema matching research using database schemas and instances. IJACSA **8**(10) (2017)
2. Ankerst, M., Breunig, M.M., Kriegel, H.P., Sander, J.: Optics: ordering points to identify the clustering structure. In: ACM SIGMOD Record, vol. 28, pp. 49–60. ACM (1999)
3. Cafarella, M.J., Halevy, A., Wang, D.Z., Wu, E., Zhang, Y.: WebTables: exploring the power of tables on the web. Proc. VLDB Endow. **1**(1), 538–549 (2008)
4. Cerda, P., Varoquaux, G., Kégl, B.: Similarity encoding for learning with dirty categorical variables. Mach. Learn. **107**(8–10), 1477–1494 (2018)
5. Charu, C.A., Chandan, K.R.: Data Clustering: Algorithms and Applications (2013)
6. De Sa, C., et al.: DeepDive: declarative knowledge base construction. ACM SIGMOD Rec. **45**(1), 60–67 (2016)
7. Ester, M., Kriegel, H.P., Sander, J., Xu, X., et al.: A density-based algorithm for discovering clusters in large spatial databases with noise (1996)
8. Gubanov, M., Priya, M., Podkorytov, M.: IntelliLIGHT: a flashlight for large-scale dark structured data (2017)
9. Gupta, R., Halevy, A., Wang, X., Whang, S.E., Wu, F.: Biperpedia: an ontology for search applications. Proc. VLDB Endow. **7**(7), 505–516 (2014)
10. Jiang, S., Liang, J., Xiao, Y., Tang, H., Huang, H., Tan, J.: Towards the completion of a domain-specific knowledge base with emerging query terms. In: 2019 IEEE 35th International Conference on Data Engineering (ICDE), pp. 1430–1441. IEEE (2019)
11. Kola, A., More, H., Soderman, S., Gubanov, M.: Generating unified famous objects (UFOs) from the classified object tables. In: IEEE Big Data, pp. 4771–4773. IEEE (2017)
12. NEXLA: An introduction to big data formats understanding Avro, Parquet, and ORC. In: NEXLA White Paper, pp. 1–12 (2018)

13. Rubenstein, D., Yin, W., Frame, M.D.: Biofluid Mechanics: An Introduction to Fluid Mechanics, Macrocirculation, and Microcirculation. Academic Press, Cambridge (2015)
14. Vohra, D.: Apache Parquet. Practical Hadoop Ecosystem, pp. 325–335. Apress, Berkeley, CA (2016). https://doi.org/10.1007/978-1-4842-2199-0_8
15. Winn, J., Guiver, J., Webster, S., Zaykov, Y., Kukla, M., Fabian, D.: Alexandria: unsupervised high-precision knowledge base construction using a probabilistic program. In: AKBC (2018)

Building Data Curation Processes
with Crowd Intelligence

Tianwa Chen[1]([⊠]), Lei Han[1], Gianluca Demartini[1], Marta Indulska[2],
and Shazia Sadiq[1]

[1] School of Information Technology and Electrical Engineering,
The University of Queensland, Brisbane, Australia
{tianwa.chen,g.demartini}@uq.edu.au, lei.han@uq.net.au,
shazia@itee.uq.edu.au
[2] Business School, The University of Queensland,
Brisbane, Australia
m.indulska@business.uq.edu.au

Abstract. Data curation processes constitute a number of activities, such as transforming, filtering or de-duplicating data. These processes consume an excessive amount of time in data science projects, due to datasets often being external, re-purposed and generally not ready for analytics. Overall, data curation processes are difficult to automate and require human input, which results in a lack of repeatability and potential errors propagating into analytical results. In this paper, we explore a crowd intelligence-based approach to building robust data curation processes. We study how data workers engage with data curation activities, specifically related to data quality detection, and how to build a robust and effective data curation process by learning from the wisdom of the crowd. With the help of a purpose-designed data curation platform based on iPython Notebook, we conducted a lab experiment with data workers and collected a multi-modal dataset that includes measures of task performance and behaviour data. Our findings identify avenues by which effective data curation processes can be built through crowd intelligence.

Keywords: Data curation · Data quality · Crowd intelligence

1 Introduction

Recent reports indicate that data scientists spend in excess of 80 percent of their time engaged in data curation activities [18]. These cost intensive, and often non value-adding, processes are considered a drain on analytics functions within organizations and result in data science project cost and time over-runs. A primary reason behind the need for data curation is the large proportion of externally acquired datasets that have different quality levels. These external datasets, sourced for example from partners, public sources, or data marketplaces, are often created for a different purpose. In fact, even internal data

N. Herbaut and M. La Rosa (Eds.): CAiSE Forum 2020, LNBIP 386, pp. 29–42, 2020.
https://doi.org/10.1007/978-3-030-58135-0_3

may have to be repurposed [25] to meet the specific needs of a certain data science project. In either case, data curation may include selection, classification, transformation, filtering, imputation, integration/fusion, or validation [8], thus requiring a variety of steps, such as format and structural transformations, meta-data extractions, annotations, de-duplication, and data categorization, to be completed before the actual analysis of the data can be performed.

Current data curation approaches can be categorized into three types, viz., ad-hoc/manual approaches [20], automated approaches [10] and crowd-sourced approaches [5]. There have been recent advances in automated approaches based on AI and machine learning techniques that have assisted in tackling certain types of data curation tasks such as relation extraction [11] and entity linking [2]. However, the bulk of data curation activities cannot feasibly and efficiently be addressed by machine-based algorithms [21] without human intervention [15]. Not surprisingly, in practice, manual approaches are still the predominant choice for data scientists [1], and thus those who need to use the data (i.e. data consumers), undertake data curation in an ad-hoc manner without following well-defined processes or guidelines e.g., they will fix an error when they encounter it during their analysis for their own benefit. Such data curation activities suffer from scalability, as well as lack of repeatability and verifiability of outcomes [6,8]. To improve the scalability of data curation, recent studies have focused on outsourcing specific data curation tasks to a crowd of data workers online. Such so-called micro-tasks, e.g. annotations of text and images, provide some benefits of scaling-out data curation, improving curation efficiency, and reducing manual data curation effort and cost. Some successful examples of crowdsourcing methods include Data Tamer [22], ZenCrowd [3] and Qurk [12].

Whereas crowd-sourced approaches work well for specific micro-tasks, they currently lack the ability to construct overall data curation processes. The involved and contextual nature of data curation activities, and the inherent complexity of the processes composed by a number of smaller tasks, make it very challenging to design, construct and validate the overall data curation process and respond to repeatability and efficiency needs in data curation. Thus, while there is promise in a crowd-sourced approach, we argue that for it to assist in reducing data curation efforts in data science projects, it needs to be extended to enable the discovery of ideal sequences of curation steps, as opposed to remaining focused at the micro-task level.

Accordingly, the aim of our study is to develop a deep understanding of how data workers engage with data curation tasks specifically related to data quality detection, and to investigate how to build repeatable and efficient data curation processes harnessing the collective intelligence of a group of data workers.

To this end, we investigate the potential of an approach that relies on human intelligence of a crowd of data workers to build data curation processes. Our study focuses on a set of tasks relating to data quality detection and tagging. We conduct a lab experiment with data workers to create a multi-modal dataset that includes measures of objective task performance and behaviour data. This unique dataset describing data worker behaviours enables us to identify patterns in their use of the available resources and to produce an effective and robust process assembled from top performers' actions.

2   Related Work

The importance and scope of data curation have increased multi-fold in the era of big data, due to the prevalence of external and re-purposed data in data science projects. Currently, three main approaches are evident in the context of data curation, namely: ad-hoc/manual, automated, and crowd-sourced approaches.

The manual approach is the most common approach [8,20], however, inherent in this approach are several issues, such as biases introduced by data users during their curation process, problems of reusability and repeatability (given the ad-hoc nature of the approach) and lack of transparency. In particular, data quality issues constitute a major challenge for data workers using a manual approach as it is likely that multiple data quality issues exist in large datasets e.g. completeness, accuracy, consistency, etc [15,23]. Recent advances in Machine Learning have improved the efficiency and scalability of automated approaches to data curation, however, issues relating to training data remain. In particular, these include the requirement for a substantial, manually labelled, training dataset for the approach to function effectively [15] and the lack of ground truth in evaluating the effectiveness of the approach [21].

A third approach, using the concept of crowd sourcing, provides a promising alternative for such situations with a potential to overcome the ad-hoc nature and lack of repeatability inherent in the manual approach. This approach aims to leverage human intelligence through outsourcing data curation micro-tasks to a crowd of data workers online. Based on the assumption that certain tasks can be performed more effectively by humans compared to algorithms, several human-in-the-loop systems (e.g., [3]) have been proposed to leverage both the scalability of machine-based data processing and the effectiveness of involving crowd intelligence [4]. However, while the approach is promising, it is plagued by challenges relating to the recruitment of a suitable crowd, determining appropriate methods to route data curation micro-tasks to the crowd [6], and the lack of comprehensive understanding of how data workers engage with data curation (required to enable appropriate routing) [6,15]. Hence, the studies aiming to better understand data worker behaviours are gaining the attention of researchers [15] and are considered crucial to improve and enable successful use of the approach.

User behaviour has been studied in many contexts. For example, understanding the behaviour of software developers has been a long-standing focus [15,19], providing insights of increasing efficiency in manipulating (source) code [14] as well as in debugging [19]. Prior research has explored how software developers work with code, in terms of their search and reuse strategies [16]. Results have shown certain behavioural patterns, for example, common copy/paste actions to replicate code snippets [16]. User behaviour has also been studied in the context of User Interface (UI) design, such as mouse scroll and keyboard behaviours to measure user satisfaction [13]. To study data workers, recent research outlined the work cycle of data scientists, ranging from discovery to design [15]. The study confirmed that the process data scientists use to clean and prepare data for analysis is time-consuming and requires data scientist's domain knowledge [15]. In addition, data workers tend to spend more time carrying out information retrieval online [14], as the ease of access to online information and open source projects has been observed to benefit their work efficiency.

In this paper, we build upon prior work in software engineering, UI design and behaviour studies of data workers to design an experiment that provides multi-modal data including performance and behaviour-log data as a means of understanding user behaviour in the context of data curation. We further note that in data science projects, data curation is a process that consists of multiple tasks. Utilizing a crowd-sourcing approach for building data curation processes from multiple crowd-sourced tasks is currently under-studied and a key objective.

3   Study Design

To evaluate data workers' behaviours, we considered a lab setting [23] for our study. The participants are asked to identify five types of data quality issues in a given dataset by writing python code to explore through a dataframe on our purposed designed platform. Participants are free to use available code snippets (which we call *DataOps* [24] throughout this paper) on the platform, and they can search for external resources using the given browser. To label identified quality issues, they need to add *tags* to each error they have discovered. The experiment commences with a pre-experiment survey, followed by a tutorial outlining definitions and examples of data quality issues and a practice example, and then they start the formal experiment whenever they feel ready. At the end of the experiment, the participants are asked to complete a post-experiment survey. The surveys based on [7] captured participant perceptions on the experiment tasks and helped ensure internal validity. In the following, we provide details of our experiment setting, instruments and participants.

Experiment Setting. To capture the interactive behaviours exhibited by participants, we design a user interface (UI) based on Jupyter Notebook (see Fig. 1). The UI of our data curation platform has three main panels: DataOps (left), the notebook (middle), and the data (right) to enable (1) viewing data-ops and their functions, (2) development of the working code, and (3) viewing data. Similar elements can be found in several data curation platforms, such as Trifacta[1], Tamr[2] [17], and Talend Open Studio[3]. We use Chrome browser extensions to inject the left and right panel on top of the notebook, and to log behavioural actions by JavaScript. Participants are only allowed to use the given browser throughout the experiment. To provide a set of internal data curation resources,

---

[1] Trifacta, https://www.trifacta.com/.
[2] Tamr Agile Data Unification and Management Systems, https://www.tamr.com/.
[3] Talend Open Studio, https://www.talend.com/products/talend-open-studio/.

Fig. 1. User interface of our experimental platform

we pre-define 21 DataOps, ranging from importing essential libraries to complex Boolean operations involving regular expressions. This set of DataOps is sufficient to complete all tasks in our experiment (i.e., participants do not necessarily need to refer to external materials in the experiment). We provide each DataOps with a description of its functionality, an explanation of how to use it (e.g., how to adjust parameters), and a code snippet that participants can copy to the notebook and use to explore the dataset and discover data quality issues. We also provide a `copy` button for each DataOps to facilitate the `copy` action. In the middle panel, we provide a standard Jupyter Notebook for participants to perform any operations (either copied from DataOps or written in Python from scratch). Because we aim at analysing the processes the participants follow to complete a given data curation task, we disabled the `cut` button in the built-in tool panel in the notebook to get a full representation of their actions. In the right panel, participants can browse the data they work with and add or remove tag labels indicating data quality issues either via the toolkit provided in the top right area of the UI or by clicking the tag labels shown in each cell in the data view. To enable smooth use of the toolkit (e.g., to add or remove tags), we disabled several hotkeys and shortcuts (e.g., "d,d", "0,0", etc.) that are pre-defined by Jupyter Notebook. The dataset that participants are asked to work with contains 13 000 records (this amount ensures writing code to perform tasks) and 4 columns including: ID, name, contact number and join date. We prepared the dataset with Parallel Data Generation Framework (PDGF)[4]. Five types of data quality issues were injected in the dataset relating to (1) missing (completeness), (2) non-unique (uniqueness), (3) duplicate (redundancy), (4) imprecise (precision) and (5) inconsistent (consistency) values. Table 1 shows definitions for these types and the number of instances injected per type.

Data Collection Instruments and Participants. In our study, we collect behaviours while participants are interacting with the experiment UI, including

---

[4] Parallel Data Generation Framework (PDGF), https://www.bankmark.de/prod ucts-and-services/.

Table 1. Data quality issues manually injected in the working dataset in formal experiment.

Type	# Instances	Definition
Missing (M)	1263	The value of a specific attribute being empty for a record
Non-unique (U)	5001	Different records identified by the same key
Duplicate (D)	5609	Multiple records being identical with respect to all attributes
Imprecise (P)	8106	Degree of accuracy for the same attribute varying across different records
Inconsistent (C)	15738 [a]	Format of the values for the same attribute varying across different records

[a] Each participant may choose one format as "standard" and thus label other formats to be inconsistent. Therefore, we present the minimum number of this type of issue to show the lower bound, where we assume the participant picks up one format that has the maximum number of instances in the dataset as "standard".

mouse clicks, copy/paste and changes between browser tabs. All behaviours are logged with a timestamp. Participation in our experiment was voluntary. All participants were undergraduate and master students in data science disciplines. In total, 39 students participated. Each was offered a $30 voucher for their time. To qualify for the experiment, participants need to have some working knowledge of Python. We do not set any restrictions on their understanding of data quality (as we cover this in the tutorial), nor did we limit the experiment duration.

4   Building a Crowd Intelligence-Based Data Curation Process

In this section, we first provide insights into individual data worker behaviours as they work through each of the five tasks aiming at identifying data quality issues. To evaluate the performance of the data workers, we use *precision, recall* and $F1$ score as the evaluation metric. For each tag in our ground truth, if it also exists in the created annotations given by the data worker (i.e. our participant), we consider it a *true positive* (tp). Otherwise, this tag is regarded as a *false negative* (fn). Similarly, for each tag created by data workers, if it does not exist in the ground truth, we consider this tag a *false positive* (fp). Therefore, by counting TPs, FPs and FNs, precision, recall and F1 could be computed by their definitions, i.e., $precision = \frac{tp}{tp+fp}$, $recall = \frac{tp}{tp+fn}$ and $F1 = 2 \cdot \frac{precision \cdot recall}{precision+recall}$. We use the observed performance and behavioural logs to build a data curation process (which we call "golden notebook"[5] throughout the paper) that assembles (parts of) the code given by best workers. We use three criteria to assess the quality of golden notebook, namely effectiveness (i.e., how many data quality issues are correctly detected), robustness (i.e., how reliable the produced golden notebook

---

[5] See http://130.102.97.188/caise20/goldenNotebook/ for our "golden notebook".

is for processing unseen data), and refinement (i.e., how well the golden notebook performs by assembling partial best code produced by different performers.).

4.1   Understanding Individual Data Curator Behaviour

Participants (indicated below through their participant ID - PID, a non- consecutive number) in our experiment work on a voluntary basis without a time limit, and hence they may or may not complete all given tasks. For this reason, to measure their performance we only consider the tasks that they have attempted.

Figure 2 shows there are 13 participants who attempted all tasks. Among them, participants P6, P14, P2, P58 and P8 are the best performers – they achieved the overall top 5 scores. Table 2 shows their detailed F1 score. From Table 3, we observe that the 5 top performers are not all ranked in the first place for all types of data quality issues. Missing and duplicate data are the top data quality issues for which most of the participants achieve a perfect score. Non-unique is the second best, and inconsistent and imprecise are the third and fourth best.

In addition, we note that 26 participants only attempted several (not all) tasks. There are 21, 14, 10, and 5 participants who did not attempt the tasks relating to the detection of imprecision, inconsistency, non-uniqueness and miss-

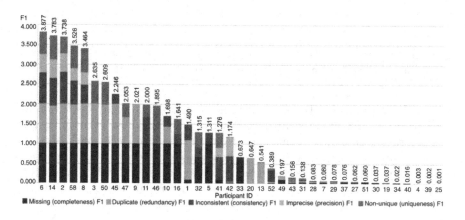

Fig. 2. Stacked value of participants' F1 score

Table 2. Top 5 performers (PIDs) and their overall performance of F1 scores

Ranking	PID	Overall score	Missing	Duplicate	Inconsistent	Non-unique	Imprecise
1	6	3.877	1.0	1.0	0.778	0.635	0.463
2	14	3.783	1.0	0.942	0.703	0.675	0.463
3	2	3.738	1.0	1.0	0.798	0.477	0.463
4	58	3.526	1.0	0.975	0.600	0.635	0.317
5	8	3.464	1.0	1.0	0.476	0.675	0.314

Table 3. Top 5 performers (PIDs) and their performance scores for each type of errors. Performers are ranked by F1 score. Notation: p: precision, r: recall, $F1$: F1 score

Ranking	Missing	Duplicate	Non-unique	Imprecise	Inconsistent
1	P2, P3, P6, P8, P9, P10, P11, P14, P16 P41, P45, P50, P58	P2, P3, P6, P8, P11	P46	P42	P2
	$p = 1.0, r = 1.0$	$p = 1.0, r = 1.0$	$p = 0.951, r = 0.847$	$p = 0.312, r = 1.0$	$p = 0.664, r = 1.0$
	$F1 = 1.0$	$F1 = 1.0$	$F1 = 0.896$	$F1 = 0.475$	$F1 = 0.798$
2	P46, P47	P45	P8, P14	P2, P6, P14	P6
	$p = 0.998, r = 1.0$	$p = 0.996, r = 1.0$	$p = 0.572, r = 0.823$	$p = 1.0, r = 0.302$	$p = 0.637, r = 1.0$
	$F1 = 0.999$	$F1 = 0.998$	$F1 = 0.675$	$F1 = 0.463$	$F1 = 0.778$
3	P5	P1	P3, P6, P50, P58	P58	P14
	$p = 1.0, r = 0.498$	$p = 0.989, r = 1.0$	$p = 0.465, r = 1.0$	$p = 0.333, r = 0.302$	$p = 0.603, r = 0.842$
	$F1 = 0.665$	$F1 = 0.995$	$F1 = 0.635$	$F1 = 0.317$	$F1 = 0.703$
4	P33	P50, P58	P2	P8	P9
	$p = 0.995, r = 0.496$	$p = 1.0, r = 0.951$	$p = 0.335, r = 0.823$	$p = 0.327, r = 0.302$	$p = 0.681, r = 0.651$
	$F1 = 0.662$	$F1 = 0.975$	$F1 = 0.477$	$F1 = 0.314$	$F1 = 0.666$
5	P49	P14	P32	P32	P42
	$p = 0.825, r = 0.052$	$p = 0.891, r = 1.0$	$p = 0.278, r = 0.847$	$p = 0.188, r = 0.301$	$p = 0.518, r = 0.844$
	$F1 = 0.098$	$F1 = 0.942$	$F1 = 0.418$	$F1 = 0.231$	$F1 = 0.642$

ing errors, respectively. Considering the effort in the coding process and lack of a break during the experiment, fatigue may have played a part in this inactivity.

Observed Behaviours. Based on the collected log data, analysis of recorded videos based on [9], and the final code written by the best performing participants, we observe their behaviours from the perspective of their strategy in tagging different data quality issues, how they interact with the three panels, how they code, search keywords in external pages, and debug when they encounter error messages. Table 4 presents further insights into the best performers' behaviour. For example, we observe that P14 wrote the least code and spent more time on external pages compared to other top-5 performers. We note that P14 made effective use of a for-loop and regular expressions to reduce the code length. Most participants copied code from previous tasks to build the next task. We also observed a unique behaviour from P58, who focused on finding all error types for each attribute, as opposed to the rest of the participants who worked to find one type of error in all of the data, before moving to the next error type.

Overall, we observed that participants viewed the dataset panel before they approached the tasks, and during coding and after tagging the data, indicating that the dataset view and browsing can provide an intuitive way for data workers to reason about the data quality issues. We note that there is no significant

Table 4. Top 5 performers interaction behaviour

Rank	PID	Time (seconds) spent on		#Change between	#Copy/paste	#Written
		Experiment pages	Other pages	Browser tabs	Action	Codes
1	6	2374	592	37	66	49
2	14	2995	1369	51	39	18
3	2	1903	510	22	62	46
4	58	2533	453	34	68	92
5	8	3320	465	21	76	66

difference in time spent on the three panels of the experiment UI across users, confirming the suitability of the design approach for the experiment UI as they all have spent a similar period on each of the three panels.

4.2 Learning from the Crowd

In this section, we outline how the collective intelligence of data workers can be harnessed. Aiming to improve the efficacy and efficiency of data curation processes, we analyzed the Python code produced by the top five performers for each type of data quality issues. Table 3 shows the top five performers and their performance (i.e., precision, recall and F1) scores for each type of error. As the top performers vary from task to task, we are able to extract (parts of) the best code snippets that work well for a particular task and assemble them to generate a collection of best code, that is, the "golden notebook" that works well for *all* tasks. By manually running the golden notebook on the same dataset as we used in the experiments, we evaluate the results from three perspectives: (i) effectiveness, where we investigate whether the results given by our golden notebook are better than those given by the best performer; (ii) robustness, where we simulate several scenarios to test if the performance of the golden notebook drops when the types of errors become more complex; and (iii) refinement, where we compute the improvement of the performance (e.g., F1) of the assembled code generated from the algorithm in a step-by-step manner. In the following, we present the construction of the golden notebook as well as the results of the evaluation.

Effectiveness. For "duplicate" and "missing" data quality issues, the participants have already reached the upper bound of F1 score (i.e., all errors of these two types were labelled correctly). Thus, to generate the golden notebook, the code given by any of these top-1 performers for the tasks is sufficient. By contrast, the highest F1 scores for "inconsistent", "imprecise" and "non-unique" were 0.798, 0.475 and 0.896, respectively (see Table 3). Therefore, a better solution for these three types of errors may be generated. In our experiment, we injected imprecise errors into two columns: *contact* and *join date*. Based on observations, some performers had worked on one column only. Table 5 shows as an example of the code given by participant "P2" and "P58" (ranked second

Table 5. Example of assemblage of top-N best code snippets and performance in terms of precision and recall for "imprecise" errors

			Individual	Assembled
ID	Code		F1	F1
P2	X = pd.to_datetime(db[db["join_date"].notnull()] ["join_date"], errors='coerce') **str**(**list**(X.loc[X.isnull ()].index.values))		0.463	0.674
P58	A = db[db["contact"].**str**.contains("^+\d\d\d{9}", na=False)] B = db[db["contact"].**str**.contains("^\d\d\d{9}", na=False)] C = db[db["contact"].**str**.contains("^0\d{9}", na=False)] db[~db.index.isin(pd.concat([A, B, C]).index)]		0.317	

and third best respectively) in solving the data quality issue of "imprecision". It is evident that P2 was investigating *join date* while P58 was dealing with problems in *contact*. Since there is no conflict between these codes, we can assemble them in the golden notebook to achieve better performance on both of the two columns. To generate the golden notebook, we start with the code given by those who achieved the highest F1 for each task. If the participant does not solve the problems for a particular column where the errors exist, we examine the code given by the next best performer. As shown in Table 5, we observe that the F1 score (performance) of the simulation result on "imprecise" has increased from 0.463 (P2) or 0.317 (P58) to 0.674 (simulation), and is better than the highest F1 on "imprecise" in the experiment (i.e., 0.475 contributed by P42, see Table 3).

Robustness. Investigating the code provided by P2 and P14, we find that both of their code works well for identifying "imprecise" errors in the column *join date*, achieving 1.0 for F1. Table 6 shows the code snippets used by these two participants to tackle the problems of "imprecision" in *join date*. We observe that P2 used `pandas.to_datetime()` while P14 used a regular expression with a specific pattern to perform the tasks. In our experiment, the task of identifying imprecise errors for *join date* requires the participants to differentiate the date format of "YYYY/MM/" from "YYYY/MM/DD". In reality, however, we may have to identify more complex imprecise errors. To understand the robustness of the code provided by the two participants, we run simulations of their code on an artificial dataset, where we randomly change 50% instances from the format of "YYYY/MM/" to "YYYYMM".

In the simulation, regular expression written by P14 can no longer match the format, and thus fails to recognize these errors. Contrary to this, the logic of code used by P2 checks a negative condition (i.e., if the condition is not satisfied, it is regarded as an error). Therefore, since `to_datetime()` function provided natively by `pandas` could not recognize "YYYY/MM/" nor "YYYYMM" as a correct date string, the recall[6] is not affected in the simulation. This shows

---

[6] P2 got 1.0 for recall while P14 got 0.5 in this simulation.

Table 6. Code snippets given by P2 and P14

P2	P14
X = pd.to_datetime(db[db["join_date"].notnull()] ["join_date"], errors='coerce') **str**(**list** (X.loc[X. isnull ()]. index.values))	regexp = re.**compile**(r'[0−9]{4}\/[0−9]{2}\/$') **for** index, cid **in enumerate**(db['join_date']): cid = **str**(cid) **if** regexp.search(cid): imprecise_list .append(index)

that writing code in negative logic has more tolerance or flexibility in matching different errors.

Refinement. Among all top-N performers, we observe that some participants have achieved high precision but low recall (e.g., P2, P6 for "imprecision", see Table 3), while others achieved high recall but low precision (e.g., P3, P6 for "non-uniqueness", see Table 3). Thus, we consider that the performance can be refined by assembling the code from those with high recall and high precision step by step. As the first step, we use the code from those who achieve the highest recall (e.g., 1.0) to select a subset of the candidates to be labelled, removing the data points where the errors do not exist[7] while keeping the maximum coverage of the issues. Then we apply the code from the one with the highest precision

Table 7. Refinement of performance by code snippets given by P6 and P46 on the identification of "non-unique" errors. Notation: p: precision, r: recall, $F1$: F1 score

ID	Code
P6 $p = 0.465, r = 1.0$ $F1 = 0.635$	db.loc [db.duplicated (['customer_id'], keep = False)]. index. tolist ()
P46 $p = 0.951, r = 0.847$ $F1 = 0.896$	dbCount = db['customer_id'].value_counts() valueList = dbCount.loc[(dbCount.values > 1)].index.tolist () dbCount2 = db.loc[db['customer_id']. isin (valueList)] dbCount3 = dbCount2['name'].value_counts() valueList = dbCount3.loc[(dbCount3.values == 1)].index.tolist() db.loc [db['name']. isin (valueList)]. index. tolist ()
Refinement (pseudo code) $p = 1.0, r = 0.847$ $F1 = 0.917$	newList = [] **for** x in P6.results : **if** (x in P46.results): newList.append(x) **print** newList # selection from P6 (subset of DB) # satisfying the conditions in P46

---

[7] In this case, we should choose the code that achieves 1.0 recall, so that the coverage of the errors can be guaranteed.

among the top-N performers (e.g., P46 for "non-uniqueness", see Table 3) to this sub-dataset, which guarantees that we only select from this subset the instances where the errors are most likely in existence. Table 7 presents an example of refinement of the performance. Among top-N performers for "non-unique" task, we use the code given by the performer with the highest recall (e.g., P6, see Table 3)[8] to generate a subset of the working dataset. Then we use the code given by P46 (who has the highest precision for this task, see Table 3) to select from this subset the data points with the errors. This process allows us to remove the instances that satisfy the condition by P46 but not covered by the results from P6 as we know that P6 has a full coverage (i.e., $recall = 1.0$) of the errors. Therefore, we can remove some data points from P46 which do not have errors. This approach results in the refinement of the performance. Table 7 shows after the refinement, the F1 score becomes 0.917, which is better than (or at least the same as) the best score individually.

5   Discussion and Conclusion

In this work we studied how data workers, using data science students as a proxy, complete data curation tasks. Collecting and analysing multi-modal data about the different processes adopted by data workers to curate data and to identify data quality issues, we have identified different possible data curation strategies and applied a systematic approach to select atomic actions from individual data workers and combine them to create an aggregated data curation process. Our results show that the approaches taken by the data workers participating in our study were often diverse and complementary in that they were able to identify different data quality issues with different levels of effectiveness and robustness. This bears implications for automatically creating aggregated data curation process through crowd intelligence. However, our work is limited as it was based on a lab experiment and we only focus on detecting data quality issues and in general data workers perform a range of data curation tasks. This work is the first step towards a systematic approach to build effective, robust and repeatable data curation processes by learning from a crowd of data workers. In further work we would conduct experiments with real crowd workers to fully test the efficiency of our proposed approach.

Acknowledgement. This work is partly supported by ARC Discovery Project DP190102141 on Building Crowd Sourced Data Curation Processes.

References

1. Azuan, N.A., Embury, S.M., Paton, N.W.: Observing the data scientist: using manual corrections as implicit feedback. In: Proceedings of the 2nd Workshop on Human-In-the-Loop Data Analytics, p. 13. ACM (2017)

---

[8] The four participants with 1.0 recall in this task (i.e., P3, P6, P50 and P58) have provided the code performing exactly the same functionality.

2. Blanco, R., Ottaviano, G., Meij, E.: Fast and space-efficient entity linking for queries. In: Proceedings of WSDM, pp. 179–188. ACM (2015)
3. Demartini, G., Difallah, D.E., Cudré-Mauroux, P.: Zencrowd: leveraging probabilistic reasoning and crowdsourcing techniques for large-scale entity linking. In: Proceedings of WWW, pp. 469–478. ACM (2012)
4. Demartini, G., Difallah, D.E., Gadiraju, U., Catasta, M., et al.: An introduction to hybrid human-machine information systems. Found. Trends® Web Sci. 7(1), 1–87 (2017)
5. Filatova, E.: Irony and sarcasm: corpus generation and analysis using crowdsourcing. In: Lrec, pp. 392–398. Citeseer (2012)
6. Freitas, A., Curry, E.: Big data curation. In: Cavanillas, J.M., Curry, E., Wahlster, W. (eds.) New Horizons for a Data-Driven Economy, pp. 87–118. Springer, Cham (2016). https://doi.org/10.1007/978-3-319-21569-3_6
7. Hart, S.G.: Nasa-task load index (NASA-TLX); 20 years later. In: Proceedings of the Human Factors and Ergonomics Society Annual Meeting, vol. 50, pp. 904–908 (2006)
8. Hey, T., Trefethen, A.: The data deluge: an e-science perspective. In: Grid computing: Making the global infrastructure a reality, pp. 809–824 (2003)
9. Jewitt, C.: National centre for research methods working paper 03/12. an introduction to using video for research. Lontoo: Institute of education (2012)
10. LeCun, Y., Bengio, Y., Hinton, G.: Deep learning. Nature 521(7553), 436–444 (2015)
11. Lin, Y., Shen, S., Liu, Z., Luan, H., Sun, M.: Neural relation extraction with selective attention over instances. In: Proceedings of the 54th Annual Meeting of the ACL (Volume 1: Long Papers), pp. 2124–2133 (2016)
12. Marcus, A., Wu, E., Karger, D.R., Madden, S., Miller, R.C.: Crowdsourced databases: Query processing with people. CIDR (2011)
13. Mehrotra, R., et al.: Deep sequential models for task satisfaction prediction. In: Proceedings of the 2017 ACM CIKM Conference, pp. 737–746 (2017)
14. Minelli, R., Mocci, A., Lanza, M.: I know what you did last summer: an investigation of how developers spend their time. In: Proceedings of the 2015 IEEE 23rd International Conference on Program Comprehension, pp. 25–35 (2015)
15. Muller, M., et al.: How data science workers work with data: discovery, capture, curation, design, creation. In: Proceedings of the 2019 CHI Conference (2019)
16. Narasimhan, K., Reichenbach, C.: Copy and paste redeemed (t). In: 2015 30th IEEE/ACM International Conference on ASE, pp. 630–640. IEEE (2015)
17. Palmer, A., Stonebraker, M., Bates-Haus, N., Cleary, L., Marinelli, M.: Getting DataOps Right. O'Reilly Media, Sebastopol (2019)
18. Patil, D.: Data Jujitsu. O'Reilly Media Inc., Sebastopol (2012)
19. Piorkowski, D.J., et al.: The whats and hows of programmers' foraging diets. In: Proceedings of the CHI Conference, pp. 3063–3072 (2013)
20. Rahm, E., Do, H.H.: Data cleaning: problems and current approaches. IEEE Data Eng. Bull. 23(4), 3–13 (2000)
21. Sadiq, S., et al.: Data quality: the role of empiricism. ACM SIGMOD Rec. 46(4), 35–43 (2018)
22. Stonebraker, M., et al.: Data curation at scale: the data tamer system. In: CIDR (2013)
23. Sutton, C., Hobson, T., Geddes, J., Caruana, R.: Data diff: interpretable, executable summaries of changes in distributions for data wrangling. In: Proceedings of the 24th ACM SIGKDD Conference, pp. 2279–2288 (2018)

24. Thusoo, A., Sarma, J.: Creating a Data-Driven Enterprise with DataOps. O'Reilly Media, Incorporated, Sebastopol (2017)
25. Zhang, R., Indulska, M., Sadiq, S.: Discovering data quality problems. Bus. Inf. Syst. Eng. **61**(5), 575–593 (2019)

R-CMMN: A Tool to Design Resilient Aware Multi-party Business Processes

Leonardo Di Paolantonio[1], Andrea Marrella[1(✉)], Massimo Mecella[1],
Barbara Pernici[2], and Pierluigi Plebani[2]

[1] Sapienza Università di Roma, Rome, Italy
dipaolantonio.1654563@studenti.uniroma1.it
{marrella,mecella}@diag.uniroma1.it
[2] Politecnico di Milano, Milan, Italy
{barbara.pernici,pierluigi.plebani}@polimi.it

Abstract. Today business organizations operate in digital ecosystems that can be conceptualized in terms of multi-party business processes, where co-operation among parties is mandatory. Being every party a potential source of failures with impacts on the entire ecosystem, resilience is a feature that should be enforced by multi-party business processes directly at design-time, to anticipate what should be done in case of possible occurring failures at run-time. In this direction, this paper presents R-CMMN, a modeling tool that implements a maturity model to support process designers in the definition of resilient aware business processes at design-time, using OMG CMMN as modeling notation.

1 Introduction

The adoption of service-oriented architectures and workflow automation has allowed information systems to become more interconnected, reducing the complexity in digitizing the communication among different organizations. As a result, every business organization operates in digital ecosystems where cooperation is mandatory [5]. Such ecosystems can be conceptualized in terms of *multi-party business processes*: every party performs some internal tasks and communicates with the other parties if some information is needed to perform the internal tasks or if some results can make the others able to perform their own tasks. While this communication increases the opportunities for the involved organizations, the side effect is that every party is a potential source of failures with impacts on the entire ecosystem. For example, a party could stop working for internal reasons and all the parties which depend on the information that the failing one is responsible for might fail as well, resulting in a domino effect.

In this context, a proper design of *resilient business processes* becomes fundamental. Resilience concerns the ability for a system to cope with unplanned situations in order to keep carrying out its mission [3]. In particular, making a multi-party business process resilient means to help the organization to cope with the complexity of the process and to avoid or mitigate possible failures

© Springer Nature Switzerland AG 2020
N. Herbaut and M. La Rosa (Eds.): CAiSE Forum 2020, LNBIP 386, pp. 43–50, 2020.
https://doi.org/10.1007/978-3-030-58135-0_4

that might affect the involved organizational structure [1]. To tackle the above challenge, in our previous works [4,6], we presented a *data-centric* approach to improve the resilience of multi-party business processes at *design-time*. The approach considers data dependencies among the involved parties, and relationships between process tasks/milestones and data are taken into account to identify the sources of possible failures, their impact, and thus improve the process model to make it resilient against these failures. To this aim, a *maturity model* for resilience awareness was proposed, based on a modeling notation extending OMG CMMN (Case Management Model and Notation). The maturity model is organized in 5 different resiliency levels, which allow designers to: *(i)* model at an increasing degree of detail how data and milestones should be defined to achieve *resilient by-design processes*, and *(ii)* quantify the distance between a process model and the complete achievement of a resiliency level.

In this paper, starting from the rigorous formalization of the maturity model provided in [4], we discuss its concrete implementation through the development of R-CMMN, a modeling tool for designing resilient by-design CMMN process models. R-CMMN not only allows us to precisely quantify the percentage of compliance of a CMMN model with respect to a specific resiliency level, but it is also able to suggest how refining a process model to reduce the possible impact of failures caused by missing or unreliable data at run-time.

The rest of the paper is organized as follows. Section 2 introduces the background to understand the tool functioning, namely an introduction to CMMN, a running example and the rationale of the maturity model. Section 3 provides an overview of the R-CMMN development and features. Finally, Sect. 4 reports some experimental results that demonstrate a good usability of the tool.

2   Background

Short Introduction to CMMN. CMMN provides a set of constructs that help the modeler to design a business process in terms of states in which the tasks can be (or cannot be) performed. The main concept of CMMN is the *case* that is defined by the *case file* (data managed in a case), the *case plan* (how the case evolves), and the *case roles* (the stakeholders). CMMN does not focus on the order in which the tasks are performed, but on the dependencies between the different states of execution of the process based on information stored in the case file. In more detail, a case plan (represented as a manila folder) is a composition of stages (represented by a rectangle shape with angled corners). The *stages* represent the episodes of a case which, in turn, could contain other stages or *tasks*, i.e., atomic units of work. Tasks and stages can be characterized by the entry and exit criteria represented by white and black diamonds. These criteria define when a task or a stage opens and when they can be considered as closed. The *milestones* (represented by ovals) express that certain intermediate goals in the case can be reached when some condition(s), modeled using entry criteria, are satisfied. Finally, *listeners* (represented by circles) represent events that might occur during the execution of the case plan and that could determine

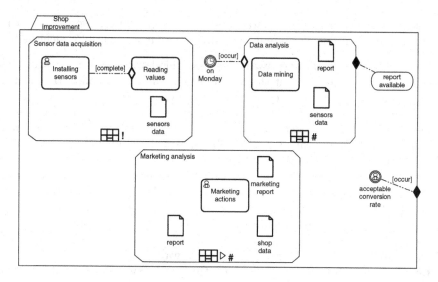

Fig. 1. CMMN diagram of the running example

the start or the end of a task or stage. Concerning the information model, CMMN simply includes the possibility to specify data objects (typical document shape) without any specific restriction on their format or content.

Running Example. Having quickly introduced the main elements of CMMN, we refer to the running example shown in Fig. 1 representing a realistic case study [6] concerning a process that collects data coming from a set of sensors. These sensors monitor the behavior of the customers inside a shop. Every week, these data are analyzed to create a report that constitutes the basis for creating marketing reports useful to identify marketing strategies (e.g., how to better distribute the items in the shelves, etc.). The case plan is composed by three main stages (i.e., Sensor data acquisition, Data analysis, and Marketing analysis). While the data analysis starts every Monday and closes when a report is produced, the other two stages always run as neither entry nor exit criteria are defined. The entire case closes when the conversion rate (the ratio between people entering into the shop with respect to the people that buy some goods) becomes acceptable for the shop owner. Finally, as defined in the sensor data acquisition stage, it is possible to express some dependencies between the tasks. In fact, the sensor reading tasks start only when the sensors have been completely installed. As previously mentioned, the information model provided by CMMN is not so rich. For this reason, we can simply add data objects to the stages to clarify which are the data that are considered when a stage is running.

Maturity Model. With the aim to classify multi-party business processes in terms of their degree of resilience awareness, the main contribution of our previous work [4] is the rigorous formalization of a maturity model that organizes

5 increasing levels of resilience awareness in a coherent framework where the actions to be taken in order to enhance the by-design resilience are identified.

- **Level 0 – No resilience awareness**. At this level, a process is designed without taking into account the data unavailability/unreliability that might cause failures during the execution. As a result, no countermeasure in case of such situations is defined. The process shown in Fig. 1 belongs to this level.
- **Level 1 — Failure awareness**. At this level, failure-aware processes are designed to have a clear map of which relevant data are subject to failures, as well as the impact of these failures.
- **Level 2 — Data resilience**. At this level, on the basis of the information about the sources of failures and their potential impacts, the designer can specify if there are alternative data sources and how to reach them.
- **Level 3 — Milestone resilience**. At this level, the designer defines, for each milestone, a new alternative milestone that represents a status that can terminate process execution in a reasonable way.
- **Level 4 — Process resilience**. At this level, based on the information about alternative data and milestones, the designer can embed in the process a recovery strategy indicating how these alternatives could be managed to improve their quality to a level that is equivalent to the original service.

3   R-CMMN

From a technical perspective, R-CMMN has been developed as a plugin of *cmmn-js*[1], an open source rendering toolkit and web modeler provided by Camunda to design CMMN 1.1 models[2]. R-CMMN is written in JavaScript, thus it can run into any modern browser requiring no server back-end. While cmmn.js provides basic features to model a CMMN process, i.e., it is based on a drag-and-drop palette to move and combine CMMN constructs into a visual workspace, with R-CMMN we have extended cmmn.js with additional features that allow designers to: *(i)* systematically increase the level of resilience of a process model, and *(ii)* quantify the distance between a process model and the complete achievement of a resiliency level. The resilient aware version of the process in Fig. 1, modeled with R-CMMN, is shown in Fig. 5. The features introduced by R-CMMN are:

(a)   (b)

Fig. 2. Connecting tasks to case file items (a) and setting criticality values to them (b)

---

1 https://bpmn.io/toolkit/cmmn-js/.
2 https://www.omg.org/spec/CMMN/1.0.

- the ability to connect case file items to tasks or event listeners (that was not possible in traditional CMMN) and specify the nature of the operations on them (e.g., create, read, predicate on, etc., cf. Fig. 2(a)). For example, in the process of Fig. 1, a designer can express the fact that the *Marketing actions* task leads to the creation of a new *marketing report* that predicates on the event listener *acceptable conversion rate* (cf. the resilient process in Fig. 5).
- the possibility to define a *criticality value* (ranging among five values, from "none" to "critical") for each case file item, to identify the data that might have more impact in case of their unavailability. For example, a designer can express that the lack of *sensors data* in the process of Fig. 1 would have a high impact on the other parties by selecting the 'H' option from the context pad of the case file item in question, which can be opened clicking on the lighting bolt icon, as shown in Fig. 2(b). The criticality value of a case file item is graphically provided through an integer number in the top left corner of its icon, with '1' meaning "maximum criticality", and '0' meaning "no criticality". Note that associating any case file item having a not-null criticality to a task is sufficient to achieve Level 1 of the maturity model.
- two additional constructs to specify *alternative case file items* and *alternative milestones*, which can be connected to their primary counterparts (with a shape identical to them, but with a dashed border) to enable the achievement of levels 2 and 3 of the maturity model, respectively (cf. Fig. 3(a) and (b)). If the designer is aware that no alternative case file item/milestone is possible for a primary one, than its icon will be explicitly labeled with an 'X'. For example, in the process of Fig. 1, two alternative sources can be defined: *public data* as an alternative to *sensors data* and the *Data mining* task, and *market analysis* to be used instead of the *report* produced by the *Marketing actions* task. Similarly, an alternative milestone *low quality report* can be coupled with the primary milestone *report available* (cf. Fig. 5).
- the possibility of defining priority chains of alternatives attached to a primary case file item or milestone. The priority of an alternative element within the chain is graphically provided through an integer number in the bottom left corner of its icon, with '1' meaning maximum priority.
- a new type of event listener, called *error event listener* (having a lightning bolt marker within the event shape), that represents the situation in which the use of an alternative case file item having a not-null criticality causes the enactment of a recovery strategy embedded in a novel type of stage, namely the *recovery stage* (having the same shape of a traditional stage, but with a

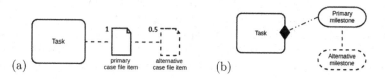

Fig. 3. Connecting alternative case file items/milestones to their primary counterparts

dashed outline). In the resilient process of Fig. 5, in case the quality of *public data* is not considered sufficient, a recovery strategy – defined by a recovery stage – is required. In our example, the goal of the recovery stage is to support the achievement of the alternative milestone *low-quality report* by providing a *Data fixing task* able to increase the *low-quality public data* in a set of revised *public data* which will be used by the *Data mining* task.

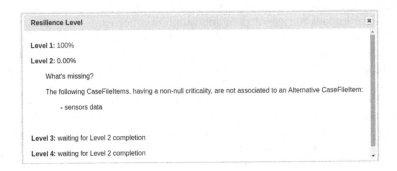

Fig. 4. Measuring the percentage of compliance with a resiliency level

In addition, for any resiliency level formalized in the maturity model, the tool enables to quantify the percentage of compliance[3] of a process model with respect to the resiliency level of interest, taking into account the different values of criticality of the modeling elements. Pushing the button "Check Level", located in the left bottom side of the workspace (cf. Fig. 5), a dialog box is shown that reports a percentage value that measures the distance between the model and the complete achievement of the next resiliency level, together with some suggestions to refine the process model towards achieving it (cf. Fig. 4).

The complete source code to setup and run R-CMMN, and a video tutorial of the tool in action, are available at: https://github.com/bpm-diag/R-CMMN.

4   User Evaluation and Conclusion

To the best of our knowledge, R-CMMN is currently the only implemented tool that allows to design process models taking into account the concept of resilience, thus no comparison was possible against other process modeling tools, being them not resilience-driven. For this reason, we opted to measure the degree of usability of the user interface (UI) developed for R-CMMN. To this aim, we employed the SUS (Software Usability Scale) questionnaire, which is one of the most widely used methodology to measure the users' perception of the usability of a tool [2]. In SUS, any statement is evaluated with a Likert scale that ranges from 1 ("strongly disagree") to 5 ("strongly agree"), and at the end of the

---

[3] The formulas to calculate the percentages of compliance with respect to any resiliency level are discussed in [4].

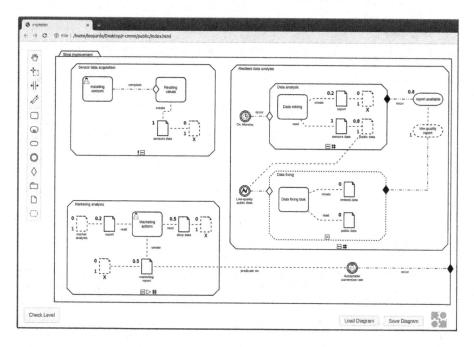

Fig. 5. The resilient aware version of the process in Fig. 1, modeled with R-CMMN

computation an overall score is assigned to the questionnaire. The score can be compared with several benchmarks presented in the research literature to determine the degree of usability of the tool being evaluated. In our test, we made use of the benchmark presented in [7], which associates to each range of the SUS score a percentile ranking varying from 0 to 100, indicating how well it compares to other 5,000 SUS observations performed in the literature.

The evaluation was enacted with a group of 16 Master students in Management Engineering during the last lecture of the course of Processes Management and Mining held in the academic year 2019/2020 at Sapienza University of Rome. Many of the students involved in the test declared to be knowledgeable (50%), skilled (12.5%) or expert (12.5%) in modeling processes with BPMN and CMMN (both the languages were covered during the course), while only the remaining 25% consider themselves as novice in process modeling.

After a preliminary short training session to introduce the concept of resilience in process modeling and describe the usage of R-CMMN, starting from the (not-resilient) process shown in Fig. 1 and its informal description, the students were requested to systematically increase its resiliency level using the features and feedback provided by the tool. All the students were able to complete their tasks within the maximum available time (20 min). As soon as a student completed the task, we administered her/him the SUS questionnaire, consisting of the traditional 10 statements typical of the original SUS [2].

	A	B	C	D	E	F	G	H	I	J	K	L	M
1	SUS Calculation												
2													
3	Participant	q1	q2	q3	q4	q5	q6	q7	q8	q9	q10	SUS Raw Score	SUS Final Score
4	p1	4	1	5	1	5	2	5	1	5	1	38,0	95
5	p2	2	3	3	4	3	4	3	3	3	4	16,0	40
6	p3	5	1	5	2	5	1	4	1	5	1	38,0	95
7	p4	5	2	5	2	5	1	5	1	4	2	36,0	90
8	p5	4	2	4	2	3	2	4	3	3	4	25,0	62,5
9	p6	4	1	5	1	4	1	5	1	4	1	37,0	92,5
10	p7	3	4	5	3	5	1	4	1	4	3	29,0	72,5
11	p8	4	1	5	2	4	3	4	3	3	1	30,0	75
12	p9	4	1	4	1	4	1	3	1	3	3	31,0	77,5
13	p10	3	2	5	1	4	2	5	1	4	3	32,0	80
14	p11	3	1	5	3	4	2	4	3	4	1	30,0	75
15	p12	3	1	5	1	5	1	5	3	3	3	32,0	80
16	p13	3	2	5	3	4	3	4	2	3	2	27,0	67,5
17	p14	4	2	5	1	4	1	4	1	5	1	36,0	90
18	p15	4	1	5	1	5	1	5	1	4	2	37,0	92,5
19	p16	5	2	5	2	4	1	5	1	5	1	37,0	92,5
20													
21												Average	79,8

Fig. 6. Computation of the SUS overall score

The collection of the ranks associated to any statement of the SUS is reported in Fig. 6, together with the SUS Final Score and the associated percentile, calculated following the procedure discussed in [7]. Since the average SUS score obtained by the tool was 79.8, according to the selected benchmark [7], the usability of the tool corresponds to a rank of A-, which indicates a degree of usability among very good and excellent.

Acknowledgments. This work has been supported by the "Dipartimento di Eccellenza" grant, the H2020 projects DESTINI and FIRST, the Italian project RoMA - Resilience of Metropolitan Areas, and the Sapienza grant BPbots.

References

1. Antunes, P., Mourão, H.: Resilient business process management: framework and services. Expert Syst. Appl. **38**(2), 1241–1254 (2011)
2. Brooke, J.: SUS: a retrospective. J. Usability Stud. **8**(2), 29–40 (2013)
3. Caralli, R.A., Allen, J.H., White, D.W.: CERT Resilience Management Model: A Maturity Model for Managing Operational Resilience. Addison-Wesley, Boston (2010)
4. Marrella, A., Mecella, M., Pernici, B., Plebani, P.: A design-time data-centric maturity model for assessing resilience in multi-party business processes. Inf. Syst. **86**, 62–78 (2019)
5. Nachira, F., Nicolai, A., Dini, P.E.A.: Digital business ecosystems. EU Commission (2007)
6. Plebani, P., Marrella, A., Mecella, M., Mizmizi, M., Pernici, B.: Multi-party business process resilience by-design: a data-centric perspective. In: Dubois, E., Pohl, K. (eds.) CAiSE 2017. LNCS, vol. 10253, pp. 110–124. Springer, Cham (2017). https://doi.org/10.1007/978-3-319-59536-8_8
7. Sauro, J., Lewis, J.R.: Quantifying the User Experience: Practical Statistics for User Research. Morgan Kaufmann, Burlington (2016)

Designing Decentralized Business Processes with Temporal Constraints

Marco Franceschetti[✉] and Johann Eder

Department of Informatics-Systems, Alpen-Adria-Universität Klagenfurt,
Klagenfurt, Austria
{marco.franceschetti,johann.eder}@aau.at

Abstract. Formulating temporal requirements and constraints in the Service Level Agreements of inter-organizational business processes raises the challenge to balance a trade-off between low coupling and expressiveness, between keeping the internals of a participating process secret and being able to express cross-organizational temporal constraints. We introduce temporal parameters as means to greatly enhance expressiveness while maintaining lean interfaces. In addition, we propose distributed procedures for checking controllability and negotiating parameter restrictions of temporally constrained inter-organizational business processes at design time, which fully respect the privacy of the local process implementations.

Keywords: Inter-organizational processes · Temporal parameters · Dynamic controllability

1 Introduction

Business applications are increasingly realized as inter-organizational processes [10,14,18,29]: several partners cooperate by composing their local processes, such that a business process emerges from the interaction of loosely coupled local processes. Typically, the implementation of local processes is kept private, and only interfaces (process views) are made available for the other parties [3].

To guarantee the effectiveness of the collaboration, contracts, in particular Service Level Agreements (SLAs), are stipulated between the business partners specifying interfaces, protocols, and service qualities. Temporal SLAs define temporal properties which need to be fulfilled, such as maximum response times, or constrain possible enactments, such as the validity period for some objects. Temporal SLAs impose restrictions on the points in time certain events may occur, and can be expressed as *temporal constraints*, i.e. sets of inequalities referring to timestamps of events.

The formulation of temporal constraints for inter-organizational processes [11], however, is restricted to the events visible in the shared interfaces (process views [3,10]) to the private local processes. It was recognized that there is a conflict between requirements to keep process internals hidden, and the need to

N. Herbaut and M. La Rosa (Eds.): CAiSE Forum 2020, LNBIP 386, pp. 51–63, 2020.
https://doi.org/10.1007/978-3-030-58135-0_5

expose internals in the interface (process view) to be able to formulate cross-organizational temporal constraints in SLAs. It is our ambition to overcome this dilemma.

Temporal variables have been introduced for the representation and communication of temporal properties of processes [8]. We propose here to exchange temporal variables in form of parameters in messages between the processes of a collaboration, and show that temporal parameters significantly increase the possibilities for formulating cross-organizational temporal constraints without exposing process internals.

Of course, it was always possible to represent temporal aspects as application data, and also to transfer these data between processes. The novel contribution, we propose, is to include these data into the time management capabilities of process design and enactment systems, i.e. to specify temporal constraints between events and data, to check the temporal correctness of process specifications at design time, and to schedule the process execution at run time, considering also these temporal parameters.

When temporal SLAs are formulated at design time, it is important to know, whether executions of the process will adhere to the temporal constraints. Dynamic controllability [6] is the suitable notion for temporal correctness, as it guarantees the fulfillment of all temporal constraints in a process under all foreseeable circumstances, even those which are not under the control of the process controller. In [8] we have shown how a single process with temporal variables can be checked for dynamic controllability. [13] addresses the problem of checking, whether a given set of requirements on the temporal variables as Temporal SLAs complies with the dynamic controllability of a service composition. For inter-organizational processes this problem is more complex, because both the design and the execution are distributed, and the values of temporal parameters are not available at process instantiation time but are communicated peu à peu during run time.

In this paper we present a model for representing interacting processes with temporal parameters. We present and discuss several typical patterns of applications, which can be formulated as temporal constraints between events of different communicating processes in an elegant way, and which would require to expose more internal details when expressed without temporal parameters. We present a procedure for checking whether a process can guarantee to meet all temporal constraints, if all temporal parameters are within their ranges agreed in the Temporal SLAs. Furthermore, we briefly sketch additional procedures for supporting process designers to negotiate admissible Temporal SLAs, in particular, acceptable range constraints for temporal parameters.

2   Motivating Example

Consider as an example the ground operations at an airport to illustrate the need to compute cross-organizational Temporal SLAs. Ground operations is an umbrella term for a large number of coordinated operations, carried out by

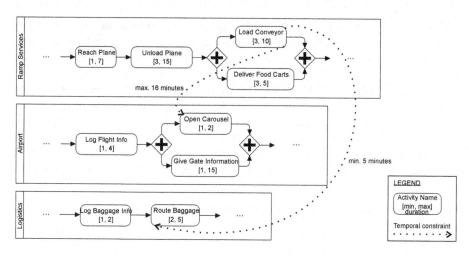

Fig. 1. Example process in BPMN-like notation with cross-organizational constraints.

several companies, from the time an airplane lands at an airport to the time it leaves it. Timeliness of operation in this context is crucial, since even one time failure may cause cascading ones, each with highly expensive penalty costs. For simplicity, we consider the interactions between 3 business partners (Fig. 1).

After an airplane has reached the gate, the checked baggage is unloaded and brought to the terminal by a ramp services company R, then loaded into a conveyor belt system (task Lc). Each piece of baggage is routed to its destination (e.g., baggage claim area, storage area, another gate) by a logistics company L. The airport company A is responsible for the baggage claim area, where a number of carousels deliver the baggage to the passengers.

L can route the baggage not earlier than 5 min after Lc, and A can deliver the baggage at most 16 min after Lc. So to coordinate and execute their processes in a timely manner, A and L need to know when Lc ended. Additionally, to schedule and verify that their processes can be executed with no time failures, they need to know in advance, the time interval in which to expect Lc to end. Here Lc^{end} is an event in the local process of R: so how to model the cross-organizational dependencies between events of R, L, and A, and how to make sure they can carry on the collaboration with timeliness guarantees? Current modeling languages require to expose the internals of the collaborating processes, for expressing the time constraints required by this scenario, and for allowing a design time check for temporal correctness of the local processes and the global one. This is not desirable, because it probably exhibits business secrets and couples the process much more tightly, complicating future changes.

Similar to the above example are other application scenarios, in which there is a need for modeling (cascading) temporal requirements in inter-organizational processes. Consider, as an example, a supply chain where some raw textile materials are delivered from India to a factory in Vietnam for some first processing, and later on the processed goods need to be transferred to a second factory in Naples, Italy via cargo ship for final processing before selling. The time window for the delivery to the first factory may heavily influence the time window for fine processing and hence selling, since cargo ships may not wait in case of delays. So the various parties would require to know the possible time windows for a correct execution, while not having to disclose their processes to each other.

So here we show how we can model the interplay of the various local temporal requirements by exchanging temporal parameters, and we show the necessity of common restrictions for actual parameter values, which guarantee no time failure will occur, without the need for any of them to expose private information.

3   Inter-organizational Process Model

3.1   Architecture, Context, and Assumptions

Inter-organizational business processes [10,18,26,29] are ensembles of communicating (local) processes executed by different parties to achieve a common (business) goal. Local processes only disclose their communication interfaces (inputs and outputs, and requirements/guarantees on them) to other parties and hide their internal process models. The involved parties are autonomous in the execution of local processes and are only bound by some form of contract (choreography, protocol, process model, and/or Service Level Agreements) [27]. In the following we assume that an inter-organizational process has already been modeled in form of a decentralized fully distributed P2P collaboration [29], and data is exchanged between local processes through message steps [18]. We focus on the definition of Temporal Service Level Agreements and on the checking of the controllability of the emerging inter-organizational processes.

Currently we target block-structured acyclic processes, to be able to reason about temporal controllability without having to cope with potential design flaws [5]. One of the local processes starts an inter-organizational process assigning a unique identifier to the process and registering the start time of the process. Other parties and their processes are instantiated by receiving a (first) message from an already activated process. For easy matching, all messages between parties include the ID of the inter-organizational and local process.

Local processes have specified task durations, deadlines, and may include additional temporal constraints stating minimum or maximum durations between events. Time is measured in an atomic time unit (chronon), like minutes, hours or days. Events will be stamped with time-points, i.e. a point on an increasing time axis representing the temporal distance to a given reference point. We call such a reference point *zero*, and assume it is global, i.e. shared between the local processes in a collaboration. All messages contain the time-point of the sending event of the message, allowing the coordination between local processes.

To formulate temporal constraints across local processes, we adopt the approach of [8], where events and time-points may be represented in temporal variables, which are exchanged as temporal parameters via messages. So temporal parameters encode process events or other time-points (e.g., the expiration date of a password), which can be communicated across the local processes in a inter-organizational process. Thus, we distinguish between input and output temporal parameters, depending on whether they are received from or sent to another local process.

Temporal parameters may be restricted through range constraints specifying minimum and maximum values for parameters. Such ranges may be used to restrict parameters to values which guarantee absence of time failures in the process, as shown in [8].

Temporal parameters allow the formulation of temporal constraints and temporal requirements between different local processes without exhibiting the involved process elements (activities, events) to other parties.

We assume that the time needed for exchanging a message is not controllable, since it depends on the connection channels between the partners. Thus, each message exchange is modeled with dedicated send and receive tasks, whose duration can only be observed to take between specified minimum and maximum values, but not controlled. We assume that these minimum and maximum values are given by, e.g., domain experts, statistical analysis, or contracts.

To avoid concurrency management and handling variables with different values over time, here we consider, without loss of generality, processes, in which each temporal parameter has exactly one writer, and may have multiple readers. The mediated transmission of a temporal parameter from its writer to a reader through another reader is possible.

While temporal parameters have been proposed also for exchanging temporal information in web services [13], the major distinction with inter-organizational processes is the time-point, when the value of temporal parameters is available. For service invocations all input parameters are instantiated, when the service is invoked. In inter-organizational processes, each message exchange may instantiate further temporal parameters, and therefore, also the value of a parameter might depend on the instantiation of other temporal parameters, and the observed durations of contingent activities [9].

3.2   Local Process Model with Temporal Parameters

Our first contribution is the formalization of a timed local process model which enables the exchange of temporal parameters to realize inter-organizational temporal constraints under the assumption presented in Sect. 3.1.

Definition 1 (Local Process Model). *A local process model P is a tuple $(proc\_id, N, E, V, C)$, where:*

- *$proc\_id$ is a unique process id.*
- *N is a set of nodes. A node n has type $n.type \in \{start, activity, xor - split, par - split, xor - join, par - join, send, receive, end\}$.*
    - *A node n with $n.type \in \{activity, send, receive\}$ has a read set $n.r$ of variables read by it, and a write set $n.w$ of variables written by it;*

- • *A node ns of type send has an additional reference ns.to to the id of the process receiving the parameter, which is in ns.r;*
- • *A node nr of type receive has an additional reference nr.from to the id of the process sending the parameter, which is in nr.w.*
- $E \subseteq N \times N$ *is a set of edges defining precedence constraints.*
- V *is a set of temporal variables, partitioned in* V^I, V^O, N^e:
  - • V^I *is the set of input parameters of* P: $V^I = \bigcup_{n:n.type=receive}\{n.w\}$;
  - • V^O *is the set of output parameters of* P: $V^O = \bigcup_{n:n.type=send}\{n.r\}$;
  - • N^e *is the set of start and end events of nodes:* $N^e = \bigcup_{n\in N}\{n^s, n^e\}$.
- C *is a set of temporal constraints consisting of*
  - • *duration constraints for each* $n \in N$: $d(n, d_{min}, d_{max})$;
  - • *range constraint for temporal variables* $v \in V^I \cup V^O$: $r(v, v_{min}, v_{max})$;
  - • *upper-bound constraints:* $ubc(a, b, \delta)$, *where* $a, b \in V, \delta \in \mathbb{N}$, *imposing that* $b \leq a + \delta$;
  - • *lower-bound constraints:* $lbc(a, b, \delta)$, *where* $a, b \in V, \delta \in \mathbb{N}$, *imposing that* $b \geq a + \delta$.

A temporal parameter is associated with a range of admissible values expressed as interval between minimum and maximum, relative to local process start time. For any process instantiation, the actual parameter value must fall within the range in order for the process to be temporally correct.

Space reasons allow only a brief informal definition, when a process is *well-formed*: we require that no admissible sequence of messages leads to a deadlock [12], that the temporal parameters are available, when they ought to be sent to other processes, and that temporal parameters are received before they are used.

Following Definition 1, for the depicted extract of the local process of R in Fig. 1: $N = \{reach, unload, load, deliver, ...\}$, $E = \{(reach, unload), (unload, deliver), (unload, load), ...\}$, $V^O = \{conv\_load\_time\}$, $N^e = \{reach^s, reach^e, ..., load^e, ...\}$, $C = \{(reach, 1, 7), ..., (load, 3, 10)\}$. One can verify that analogous sets represent, e.g., the process of L, with the additional constraint expressing the minimum 5 min to elapse between conveyor loading time at R and routing start at L $lbc(conv\_load\_time, route^s, 5)$. Expressing this constraint requires a send, resp. receive task in R, resp. L (not depicted in Fig. 1), for transmitting the conveyor belt loading time encoded in parameter $conv\_load\_time$.

3.3 Local Process in an Inter-organizational Process

For broader generality, we assume that a local process which takes part into an inter-organizational process has a local view of the global process. This means that a local process P_i, only sees the direct exchanges of temporal parameters between P_i and any other local process P_j, but not parameter exchanges between P_j and a third process P_k.

Temporal parameters are used in temporal constraints in different local processes. Thus, avoiding that these constraints are violated requires that the parameters take only values which are allowed by all processes using them, and are exchanged at agreed times as well. However, also the time in which a parameter exchange occurs can be modeled through parameters. So the exchange of temporal parameters requires a number of restrictions on the temporal parameters values, on which all the interested process partners agree.

If a set of parameter restrictions is given, each local process can verify, whether these restrictions allow for temporally correct executions. However, often not all restrictions are known, and they must be computed. Thus, a meta-protocol for negotiating adequate parameter restrictions between communicating processes is required. We discuss the implications and problems to address to this end in Sect. 4.

3.4 Application Patterns

The process model we propose enables the expression of a number of application patterns for cross-organizational temporal constraints and dependencies without exhibiting process internals. For validating the increase in expressiveness, we show some application patterns with examples, which could not be expressed with current models for temporal constraints.

- *Best before date:* Consider an upper bound constraint $ubc(s, d, \delta)$ between events of different local processes. The first process can encode $t_s + \delta$ in a temporal variable, say D, and eventually send it to the other process. The other process can encode a constraint $ubc(D, d, 0)$.

  Example: A process generates a one-time password, which is valid until a time-point D for invoking some service S. The receivers includes an upper-bound constraint $ubc(D, call\_S, 0)$ to restrict the call of service S to happen before time point D.

  We would not know, how to formulate such a constraint in current process models. In particular, the receiver does not need to know about the activity generating the password and the sender does not need to know about the activity using the password. This pattern can be generalized that a sender might restrict when the receiver may perform some activities.
- *Best before date - receiver:* A process p_s may transmit to some other process p_r the timestamp of occurrence of some local event, which may be used to constrain some activity at p_r, without exposing the internals of p_s or p_r.

  Example 1: A blood sample is sent to the lab together with the timestamp, when the blood was extracted: for each possible test, the lab can include an upper-bound constraint, until which time-point after the extraction it can be performed.

  Example 2: In the example of Fig. 1, $t = Lc^e$ can be sent to L and A to constrain the execution times of Rb and Oc with $lbc(t, Rb^s, 5)$ and $ubc(t, Oc^s, 16)$.

– *Responding to time requests:* A process p_r may receive a temporal parameter and is asked to respond with the time in which some (local) event is expected to occur as a consequence of the received timestamp.

Example: Since a clearing process might involve fixed-date constraints, a hiring process might ask, when it has to submit a request to receive the result before a given date.

– *Mediating between not directly communicating processes:* As temporal parameters are data which can be transitively transmitted, temporal constraints can be established between activities of processes, which do not directly communicate: a mediator process p_m may be used to forward some temporal parameter received from an origin process p_o to a destination process p_s.

Example: A real estate agent might send the deadline of a binding offer of a potential buyer to the seller.

All these patterns and examples have in common, that the cross-organizational constraints they induce could not be formulated with current temporal models without exposing additional information about the local processes to maybe also additional parties. Thus we can conclude, that the proposed model increases the expressiveness for modeling time constrained inter-organizational processes.

4   Temporal Correctness

4.1   Dynamic Controllability of Local Processes

In recent years *dynamic controllability* (see [6]) was established as the most important notion for checking temporally constrained processes. A process is dynamically controllable, if the process controller has a dynamic execution strategy that the process can be executed without violating any temporal constraint despite uncertainties due to uncontrollable durations. The execution strategy assigns start times to process steps dynamically in response to the observation of actual durations observed at run time.

Most approaches for checking dynamic controllability of local processes are based on a mapping to equivalent temporal networks, such as Simple Temporal Networks with Uncertainty (STNUs) as we showed in [8]. Basically, these networks are oriented graphs with nodes representing time-points, and edges representing temporal constraints between time-points. Edges may be contingent or non-contingent. A contingent edge represents a constraint which cannot be controlled: the value of the time-point target of such an edge can only be observed (within the interval specified by the edge weight). A non-contingent edge represents a constraint, which can be controlled by assigning to its target time-point a value compatible with the bound specified in the edge weight.

In a nutshell: for each process step there is a pair of STNU nodes, one for the start and one for the end event of the step. These nodes are connected by STNU edges representing the step duration. Precedence constraints and lower- and upper-bound constraints are mapped into STNU non-contingent edges.

Additionally, the network has one node for each temporal parameter. Each input parameter is mapped to a contingent node and is connected to Z, the STNU zero time-point, by contingent edges with weight the parameter range, since it comes with an assigned value on which the process controller cannot have any influence. In contrast, each output parameter is connected to Z with non-contingent edges weighted with the range of the parameter. All parameters are used in temporal constraints, which link them to some process event.

A process is dynamically controllable, if and only if its equivalent STNU is dynamically controllable. In [8] we have shown that, to verify the dynamic controllability of a process, we map it into an equivalent STNU, and apply existing techniques for the dc-check of STNUs. Due to space reasons, we refer to [8] for a detailed presentation of the approach to checking dynamic controllability of local processes with temporal parameters based on the STNU mapping.

4.2 Temporal Properties of Inter-organizational Processes

A timed inter-organizational process is a process emerging from the collaboration of local processes exchanging temporal parameters. It is dynamically controllable if all its local processes are dynamically controllable. A local process is dynamically controllable, if it has an execution strategy, such that for all possible values of input parameters all temporal constraints can be satisfied.

We propose a series of procedures for checking the temporal properties of inter-organizational processes at design time and the monitoring of temporal constraints at run time. Furthermore, we propose procedures to supporting the design and the negotiation of temporal constraints in the choreography, in particular, the admissible ranges of temporal parameters.

- Checking of dynamic controllability for a choreography specification;
- Forward propagation of constraints: computing the smallest ranges for output parameters given ranges of input parameters;
- Backward computation of constraints: computing largest possible ranges for input parameters given the ranges of output parameters;
- Completion of choreography specifications: compute the missing parameter ranges given a partial specification of parameter ranges;
- Negotiation of parameter ranges: computing the trade-offs between ranges of different parameters to support the negotiation of ranges between the parties of an inter-organizational process.

All these procedures require a meta-communication framework for the involved parties to exchange the choreography specifications. They are based on computing derived constraints between the variables of a temporal constraint network (STNU, resp. CSTNU [17]) representing the time-points of events of a process execution, or the temporal parameters.

5 Related Work

A consistent body of research is devoted to time management for business processes: general overviews of related works in the area can be found in [4,7,11].

The problem of checking whether deadlines and time constraints can be fulfilled in time-constrained process definitions is addressed by early works such as [1,24]. The techniques adopted in these works are based on network analysis, scheduling, or constraint networks. Further works such as [2,15] address the case of inter-organizational processes and service compositions, while [20] analyzes the representation and support of temporal constraints in modularized processes. However, none of these approaches considers using temporal variables for expressing temporal properties or requirements, which, as we show here, increase the expressiveness for temporal constraints without affecting secrecy.

Towards the use of temporal variables is the work in [19], which aims at conceding controlled violations of temporal constraints by checking temporal consistency at both design- and run time. The use of variables, however, is limited to the definition of controlled violations of temporal constraints, and variables are also not explicitly defined in the process model.

The formalization of time patterns and their semantics in [21] brought a much needed consolidation in the area of representing temporal constraints for process models. Time patterns categorize temporal constraints by defining 10 categories, based on temporal properties of events derived from control flow. Temporal variables allow to extend this work by enabling new constraints.

For time-constrained process models there is also the need for pro-active monitoring of the compliance of process instances to their process model, which is considered in, e.g., [16,22]. [23] uses timed automata and model checking techniques for the analysis of properties of collaborative processes. However, to the best of our knowledge, all these approaches consider satisfiability rather than dynamic controllability as the notion for temporal correctness.

Here we showed an algorithm for computing missing constraints on variables, which is based on the flow of messages exchanging these variables. Of course one may use process mining techniques [28] to derive missing temporal qualities for a model; however, this is only possible if there is a sufficient number of traces available in the process logs. In contrast, here we focus on new process definitions, and on a design time check of their temporal properties.

As for dynamic controllability check, we rely on an approach based on mapping process definitions to Simple Temporal Networks with Uncertainty (STNUs) [25]. Considerable research efforts have been devoted in the last decades both to developing different notions of controllability for temporal constraint networks, and to developing more expressive network models [17,20,30,31]. Considering the increasing complexity for verifying dynamic controllability of these more refined networks, we regard STNUs as a suitable formalism for representing the temporal dimension of a process model and deriving missing temporal information at design time.

6 Conclusions

Service Level Agreements including temporal obligations are crucial for the definition of business collaborations. However, the need for secrecy has frequently precluded the formulation of inter-organizational temporal constraints. The introduction of temporal variables opens interesting new ways to define inter-organizational processes with Temporal SLAs, as process parties might exchange temporal information as data without jeopardizing the secrecy of process models.

We introduced a process model for decentralized business processes in which temporal constraints are realized by the exchange of such parameters. The proposed process model allows the expression of a number of application patterns which would require exhibiting process internals otherwise.

This work is a first step in the design of time-constrained inter-organizational processes with guarantees of confidentiality and temporal correctness. As future work we intend to carry out a systematic investigation of application patterns, and design and implement the proposed procedures to support the negotiation of parameter restrictions.

References

1. Bettini, C., Wang, X., Jajodia, S.: Temporal reasoning in workflow systems. Distrib. Parallel Databases **11**(3), 269–306 (2002)
2. Cardoso, J., Sheth, A., Miller, J., Arnold, J., Kochut, K.: Quality of service for workflows and web service processes. J. Web Semant. **1**(3), 281–308 (2004)
3. Chebbi, I., Dustdar, S., Tata, S.: The view-based approach to dynamic inter-organizational workflow cooperation. Data Knowl. Eng. **56**(2), 139–173 (2006)
4. Cheikhrouhou, S., Kallel, S., Guermouche, N., Jmaiel, M.: The temporal perspective in business process modeling: a survey and research challenges. SOCA **9**(1), 75–85 (2014). https://doi.org/10.1007/s11761-014-0170-x
5. Combi, C., Gambini, M.: Flaws in the flow: the weakness of unstructured business process modeling languages dealing with data. In: Meersman, R., Dillon, T., Herrero, P. (eds.) OTM 2009. LNCS, vol. 5870, pp. 42–59. Springer, Heidelberg (2009). https://doi.org/10.1007/978-3-642-05148-7_6
6. Combi, C., Posenato, R.: Controllability in temporal conceptual workflow schemata. In: Dayal, U., Eder, J., Koehler, J., Reijers, H.A. (eds.) BPM 2009. LNCS, vol. 5701, pp. 64–79. Springer, Heidelberg (2009). https://doi.org/10.1007/978-3-642-03848-8_6
7. Combi, C., Pozzi, G.: Temporal conceptual modelling of workflows. In: Song, I.-Y., Liddle, S.W., Ling, T.-W., Scheuermann, P. (eds.) ER 2003. LNCS, vol. 2813, pp. 59–76. Springer, Heidelberg (2003). https://doi.org/10.1007/978-3-540-39648-2_8
8. Eder, J., Franceschetti, M., Köpke, J.: Controllability of business processes with temporal variables. In: Proceedings of the 34th ACM/SIGAPP Symposium on Applied Computing, pp. 40–47. ACM (2019)
9. Eder, J., Franceschetti, M., Köpke, J., Oberrauner, A.: Expressiveness of temporal constraints for process models. In: Woo, C., Lu, J., Li, Z., Ling, T.W., Li, G., Lee, M.L. (eds.) ER 2018. LNCS, vol. 11158, pp. 119–133. Springer, Cham (2018). https://doi.org/10.1007/978-3-030-01391-2_19

10. Eder, J., Kerschbaumer, N., Köpke, J., Pichler, H., Tahamtan, A.: View-based interorganizational workflows. In Proceedings of the 12th International Conference on Computer Systems and Technologies, pp. 1–10. ACM (2011)
11. Eder, J., Panagos, E., Rabinovich, M.: Workflow time management revisited. Seminal Contributions to Information Systems Engineering, pp. 207–213. Springer, Heidelberg (2013). https://doi.org/10.1007/978-3-642-36926-1_16
12. Elmagarmid, A.K.: A survey of distributed deadlock detection algorithms. ACM Sigmod Rec. **15**(3), 37–45 (1986)
13. Franceschetti, M., Eder, J.: Checking temporal service level agreements for web service compositions with temporal parameters. In: 2019 IEEE International Conference on Web Services (ICWS), pp. 443–445. IEEE (2019)
14. Grefen, P., Hoffner, Y.: Crossflow-cross-organizational workflow support for virtual organizations. In: Proceedings Ninth International Workshop on Research Issues on Data Engineering: Information Technology for Virtual Enterprises. RIDE-VE 1999, pp. 90–91. IEEE (1999)
15. Guermouche, N., Godart, C.: Timed model checking based approach for web services analysis. In: ICWS 2009. IEEE International Conference on Web Services, 2009, pp. 213–221. IEEE (2009)
16. Hashmi, M., Governatori, G., Lam, H.-P., Wynn, M.T.: Are we done with business process compliance: state of the art and challenges ahead. Knowl. Inf. Syst. **57**(1), 79–133 (2018). https://doi.org/10.1007/s10115-017-1142-1
17. Hunsberger, L., Posenato, R., Combi, C.: The dynamic controllability of conditional STNS with uncertainty. arXiv preprint arXiv:1212.2005 (2012)
18. Köpke, J., Franceschetti, M., Eder, J.: Optimizing data-flow implementations for inter-organizational processes. Distrib. Parallel Databases **37**(4), 651–695 (2018). https://doi.org/10.1007/s10619-018-7251-3
19. Kumar, A., Barton, R.R.: Controlled violation of temporal process constraints-models, algorithms and results. Inf. Syst. **64**, 410–424 (2017)
20. Lanz, A., Posenato, R., Combi, C., Reichert, M.: Controlling time-awareness in modularized processes. In: Schmidt, R., Guédria, W., Bider, I., Guerreiro, S. (eds.) BPMDS/EMMSAD -2016. LNBIP, vol. 248, pp. 157–172. Springer, Cham (2016). https://doi.org/10.1007/978-3-319-39429-9_11
21. Lanz, A., Reichert, M., Weber, B.: Process time patterns: a formal foundation. Inf. Syst. **57**, 38–68 (2016)
22. Ly, L.T., Maggi, F.M., Montali, M., Rinderle-Ma, S., van der Aalst, W.M.: Compliance monitoring in business processes: functionalities, application, and tool-support. Inf. Syst. **54**, 209–234 (2015)
23. Mallek, S., Daclin, N., Chapurlat, V., Vallespir, B.: Enabling model checking for collaborative process analysis: from bpmn to 'network of timed automata'. Enterp. Inf. Syst. **9**(3), 279–299 (2015)
24. Marjanovic, O., Orlowska, M.E.: On modeling and verification of temporal constraints in production workflows. Knowl. Inf. Syst. **1**(2), 157–192 (1999)
25. Morris, P.H., Muscettola, N.: Temporal dynamic controllability revisited. In: AAAI, pp. 1193–1198 (2005)
26. van der Aalst, W.M.: Process-oriented architectures for electronic commerce and interorganizational workflow. Inf. Syst. **24**(8), 639–671 (1999)
27. Van Der Aalst, W.M., Lohmann, N., Massuthe, P., Stahl, C., Wolf, K.: Multiparty contracts: agreeing and implementing interorganizational processes. Comput. J. **53**(1), 90–106 (2010)
28. van der Aalst, W.M., Schonenberg, M., Song, M.: Time prediction based on process mining. Inf. Syst. **36**(2), 450–475 (2011)

29. van der Aalst, W.M.P., Weske, M.: The P2P approach to interorganizational work-flows. In: Dittrich, K.R., Geppert, A., Norrie, M.C. (eds.) CAiSE 2001. LNCS, vol. 2068, pp. 140–156. Springer, Heidelberg (2001). https://doi.org/10.1007/3-540-45341-5_10

30. Vidal, T.: Handling contingency in temporal constraint networks: from consistency to controllabilities. J. Exp. Theoret. Artif. Intell. 11(1), 23–45 (1999)

31. Zavatteri, M., Viganò, L.: Conditional simple temporal networks with uncertainty and decisions. Theoret. Comput. Sci. 797, 77–101 (2019)

Seed Model Synthesis for Testing Model-Based Mutation Operators

Pablo Gómez-Abajo[1]([⊠]), Esther Guerra[1], Juan de Lara[1],
and Mercedes G. Merayo[2]

[1] Modelling and Software Engineering Group,
Universidad Autónoma de Madrid, Madrid, Spain
{Pablo.GomezA,Esther.Guerra,Juan.deLara}@uam.es
http://miso.es
[2] Design and Testing of Reliable Systems Group,
Universidad Complutense de Madrid, Madrid, Spain
mgmerayo@fdi.ucm.es
http://antares.sip.ucm.es/testing/

Abstract. In software engineering, *mutation* consists in injecting small changes in artefacts – like models, programs, or data – for purposes like (mutation) testing, test data generation, and all sorts of search-based methods. These activities normally require the definition of sets of mutation operators, which are often built ad-hoc because there is currently poor support for their development and testing.

To improve this situation, in previous work we proposed a model-based approach to create and execute mutation operators. Our proposal represents the artefacts to be mutated as models and provides a domain-specific language called WODEL to define the mutation operators. However, testing the operators is cumbersome, since it requires the manual creation of input seed models. To facilitate this testing process, we propose a method – based on model finding – for the automated synthesis of test models that exercise the defined mutation operators. We provide tool support for our proposal, and illustrate its usage by defining mutation operators for BPMN.

Keywords: Model-based mutation · Model-driven engineering · Model synthesis · OCL · WODEL · BPMN

1 Introduction

Mutation consists in the selective introduction of modifications into sets of seed artefacts, like models, programs or data. Mutation is at the core of many techniques in software engineering, like mutation testing (where programs are mutated with faults to evaluate the quality of a test suite) [5,14], test data generation (like in mutation-based fuzzing, which introduces small changes to existing test inputs) [26], and search-based software engineering (which applies

© Springer Nature Switzerland AG 2020
N. Herbaut and M. La Rosa (Eds.): CAiSE Forum 2020, LNBIP 386, pp. 64–76, 2020.
https://doi.org/10.1007/978-3-030-58135-0_6

metaheuristic search techniques to software engineering problems, where candidate solutions are combined and mutated) [15]. Mutation has also been applied for other purposes, like the automatic generation of exercises and quizzes [9] or testing distributed applications in simulated environments [3].

Mutation-based methods require the creation of mutation operators able to change the target artefacts in pertinent ways. For example, for mutation testing, operators need to emulate common faults made by competent developers. Such operators are typically defined over the abstract syntax tree of the program, which makes them difficult to test since the input data of the operators are programs. Moreover, operators are often defined ad-hoc using general programming languages not designed for mutating artefacts, like Java [19] or C [18], which is costly and error-prone.

To improve this situation, we propose an approach to facilitate the creation and testing of mutation operators. It is model-based to enable its application to heterogeneous artefacts (programs, models, data). This means that the artefacts to mutate are represented as models conforming to a meta-model, for which we rely on injection (artefact-to-model) and extraction (model-to-artefact) transformations. Our solution includes a domain-specific language (DSL) called WODEL [8,9] specially tailored to design mutation operators applicable over models. To help in the validation of the designed operators, we offer facilities for synthesizing models over which the operators can be tested. Such models are ensured to provide full statement coverage of the mutation program.

Our method is supported by the WODEL tool [10]. While the DSL WODEL was introduced in [8,9], in this paper we focus on the facility for seed model synthesis, based on constraint solving and model finding [20].

The rest of this paper is organized as follows. Section 2 introduces a running example in the area of process modelling. Then, Section 3 describes the WODEL DSL. Section 4 explains our methods to synthesize models for testing mutation operators, and Sect. 5 describes our current tool support. Finally, Sect. 6 reviews related work, and Sect. 7 concludes the paper.

2   Running Example: Mutation for Process Models

A number of research works have applied mutation to workflow languages for different purposes, like evaluating the quality of test cases (as in [7] for WS-BPEL), optimising process models (as in [16] for BPMN), or for process mining using a genetic approach (as in [6] for process trees or [22] for Petri nets). As an illustration, in this paper, we are defining a set of mutation operators for the Business Process Model and Notation (BPMN)[1].

Figure 1 shows part of a simplified BPMN meta-model taken from an editor built by a third-party[2]. A process defines a set of FlowObjects, which can be either Activities (i.e., a work to be done), Events (to denote that something happens, such as the start or end of the process), or Gateways (to fork or merge several paths).

---

[1] http://www.bpmn.org/.

[2] https://github.com/bluezio/simplified-bpmn-example.

Depending on the kind of gateway, the execution of its outgoing paths can be in parallel (AND), inclusive (OR, one or more paths are executed), or exclusive (XOR, only a path is executed). The OCL invariant inv2 ensures that gateways always have input and output paths. Finally, flow objects can be connected through ConnectingObjects to specify the execution flow (Sequence), send messages (Message), or associate artefacts to flow objects (Association). The OCL invariant inv1 ensures that start events have no input flows, end events have no output flows, and flow objects are not connected to themselves. To better illustrate model synthesis in Sect. 4, we have restricted processes to have between 1 and 10 elements, as cardinality of reference BusinessProcess.elements indicates.

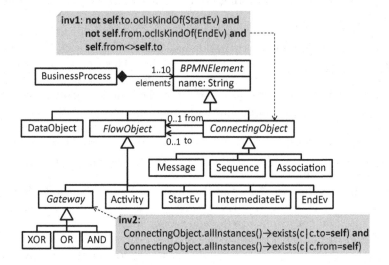

Fig. 1. Simplified BPMN meta-model.

Figure 2 shows a simple BPMN model in concrete syntax. It describes the process to satisfy someone who is hungry. The process starts when a person becomes hungry. The first activity is to buy food, followed by cooking the food. Then, when the meal is ready, the person eats it, and this concludes the process.

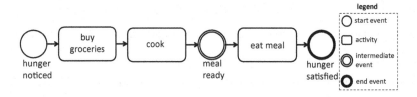

Fig. 2. An example BPMN model (using the standard concrete syntax).

In the next section, we introduce our DSL WODEL for model mutation, and use it to define a set of mutation operators for BPMN.

3   Wodel: A Domain Specific Language for Model Mutation

WODEL [8,9] is a DSL for the specification of mutation operators. It is domain-independent, and so it can be applied to arbitrary languages, or to other kinds of artefacts like data. For this purpose, it relies on the provision of a domain meta-model specifying the structure of the artefacts to be mutated. The execution of a WODEL program yields a set of mutant models obtained by applying the specified operators to a set of given seed models, using different policies. For traceability, a registry with the mutations used to generate each mutant is also produced. WODEL ensures that the created mutant models conform to the domain meta-model and satisfy its OCL invariants.

WODEL provides mutation primitives to *select, modify, create, delete, clone* and *retype* objects; and to *create, modify* and *delete* references. Its mutation engine has built-in functionalities to ease the definition of mutation operators; for example, new objects are automatically added to a suitable container reference, and mandatory attributes and references without an explicit value are automatically initialized. Its editing environment [10] features code completion, type checking, and generation of stand-alone Java code from WODEL programs (cf. Sect. 5). The tool can be extended with post-processing applications. Two examples are the framework for the automated generation of exercises presented in [9], and the mutation testing development framework introduced in [11].

Listing 1 shows a simple WODEL program for defining a mutation operator for BPMN. Line 1 specifies the strategy for mutant synthesis: generating either a maximum number of mutants, or all possible ones by using the keyword exhaustive. Line 2 states the output folder to store the mutants, and the input folder with the seed models. Line 3 configures the meta-model in use (we use the on in Fig. 2). The remainder of the program defines the mutation operators.

```
1  generate exhaustive mutants
2  in "out/" from "model/"
3  metamodel "http://bpmn.com"
4
5  with blocks {
6    ev2ac {
7      retype
8        one [StartEv, IntermediateEv, EndEv]
9        as Activity
10   }
11 }
```

Listing 1. Defining a mutation operator for BPMN with WODEL.

In this example, the operator ev2ac retypes an event of any kind into an activity (lines 7–9). This operator uses a single mutation primitive, but in general, operators can use any number of mutation statements. For instance, Table 2 in the appendix contains other more complex operators for BPMN, both proposed in the literature [21] and created by us. Mutation primitives can be scheduled to be applied a random number of times within a given interval. If they do not define an interval (as in the example), they are applied just once.

Figure 3 shows an application of the mutation operator in Listing 1 to the BPMN model of Fig. 2. In the resulting mutant, the IntermediateEv 'meal ready' is replaced by an equally named Activity, and the incoming/outgoing references are preserved by the operator.

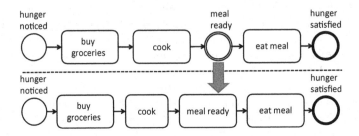

Fig. 3. Application of the mutation operator in Listing 1 to a BPMN model.

4 Seed Model Synthesis Using Model Finding

As any other software, mutation programs need be tested to detect possible errors, so that they can be fixed. In the case of WODEL, this implies the creation of test models upon which the mutation programs can be executed. However, creating test models manually is tedious and error-prone, and it is difficult to ensure a full coverage of the program.

Therefore, to ease the testing of WODEL programs and operators, we propose a method based on model finding [17] to automatically produce seed models over which all instructions of the given WODEL program are applicable (if such models exist in the given search scope).

Figure 4 outlines the seed model synthesis process. It relies on model search, a technique which applies constraint resolution over models [17]. In particular, the synthesizer enriches the description of the domain meta-model and its invariants with additional OCL constraints derived from the WODEL program. These constraints express the requirements that a seed model must fulfil to allow the application of each mutation operator included in the program. Next, the enriched meta-model is loaded into a model finder [20], which performs a bounded search of instances of the meta-model satisfying the OCL constraints. If a model is found, then it ensures full statement coverage of the WODEL program when executed with the model.

Table 1 shows the templates used to generate the OCL constraints for each mutation primitive, as well as illustrative examples. For instance, the OCL template for the object deletion primitive demands the existence of an object with the specified type and feature values, and included in a container reference that would not violate its lower cardinality bound if the object deletion takes place.

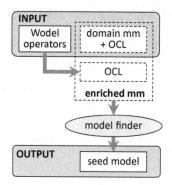

Fig. 4. Process for automated model synthesis.

The table shows as an example the deletion of an Activity: the derived OCL constraint checks that there exists some Activity, and the BusinessProcesses to which it belongs contain other elements apart from the Activity (i.e., the size of reference BusinessProcess.elements is bigger than 1, and deleting the Activity would still satisfy the reference cardinality).

Other OCL templates deal with object creation (which requires the existence of a suitable container reference with enough space for the object), object cloning (which in addition requires the existence of a candidate object to be cloned), object retyping (which requires conditions equivalent to those for deleting and creating objects for every container or regular reference that is not source- or target-compatible with the new type), reference modification (which requires the existence of an object of the target class), reference creation (which in addition requires a reference with space to add the object of the target class), and reference deletion (which requires that the reference fulfils its lower cardinality after taking one of its objects out).

For readability reasons, Table 1 shows the template associated to one occurrence of a mutation primitive. However, a program may apply the same primitive with the same parameters more than once. This may occur because the primitive is repeated, or because it defines an interval of applications bigger than one. Hence, in the general case, we count how many times a same instruction appears (i.e., is to be executed), and generate a slightly more complex constraint where each such occurrence is represented as a variable. For instance, if the mutation create Activity has to occur twice, we generate the constraint shown in Listing 2 (cf. Table 1).

BusinessProcess.allInstances()→exists(b1,b2 |
   (b1 <> b2 and b1.elements→size() < 10 and b2.elements→size() < 10)
   or b1.elements→size() < 9)

Listing 2. OCL invariant derived from a WODEL program creating two activities.

Table 1. Templates to generate OCL constraints from mutation primitives.

Conditions to check	OCL template	Example
Object filter: Auxiliary template used to check that an object has the given feature values.	$o.\langle feat_1\rangle = \langle val_1\rangle$ ... **and** $o.\langle feat_n\rangle = \langle val_n\rangle$	
Object selection, object modification: There is an object with the given type and feature values.	$\langle Class\rangle$.**allInstances()** $\rightarrow$**exists**(o | $\langle object-filter\rangle$)	**Wodel:** **modify one** Activity **where** {name = 'InitialName'} **with** {name = 'ModifiedName'} **OCL:** Activity.**allInstances()** $\rightarrow$**exists**(a | a.name = 'InitialName')
Object creation: There is a container reference of the object's type with space to add more objects.	$\langle Container\rangle$.**allInstances()** $\rightarrow$**exists**(o | o.$\langle ref\rangle$$\rightarrow$**size()** < $\langle upB\rangle$))	**Wodel:** a = **create** Activity **OCL:** BusinessProcess.**allInstances()** $\rightarrow$**exists**(b | b.elements$\rightarrow$**size()** < 10)
Object deletion: There is an object with the given type and feature values, and its deletion does not violate the lower bound of any reference of the object's type.	$\langle Class\rangle$.**allInstances()** $\rightarrow$**exists**(o | $\langle object-filter\rangle$ **and** $\langle Container\rangle$.**allInstances()** $\rightarrow$**forAll**(c | c.$\langle ref\rangle$$\rightarrow$**includes**(o) **implies** c.$\langle ref\rangle$$\rightarrow$**size()** > $\langle lowB\rangle$))	**Wodel:** **remove one** Activity **OCL:** Activity.**allInstances()**$\rightarrow$**exists**(a | BusinessProcess.**allInstances()** $\rightarrow$**forAll**(b | b.elements$\rightarrow$**includes**(a) **implies** b.elements$\rightarrow$**size()** > 1))
Object cloning: There is an object with the given type and feature values, and a container reference of that type with space to add more objects.	$\langle Class\rangle$.**allInstances()** $\rightarrow$**exists**(o | $\langle object-filter\rangle$) **and** $\langle Container\rangle$.**allInstances()** $\rightarrow$**exists**(o | o.$\langle ref\rangle$$\rightarrow$**size()** < $\langle upB\rangle$)	**Wodel:** **deep clone one** Sequence **OCL:** Sequence.**allInstances()** $\rightarrow$**exists**(s | true) **and** BusinessProcess.**allInstances()** $\rightarrow$**exists**(b | b.elements$\rightarrow$**size()** < 10)
Object retyping: There is an object with the given source type and feature values. If the target type is not compatible with the container of the source type, conditions to delete a source object and create a target one are required (and similar for refs not compatible with target type). Orcatenate for each considered source/target type.	$\langle Class\rangle$.**allInstances()** $\rightarrow$**exists**(o | $\langle object-filter\rangle$ **[and** $\langle SrcContainer\rangle$.**allInstances()** $\rightarrow$**forAll**(c | c.$\langle ref\rangle$$\rightarrow$**includes**(o) **implies** c.$\langle ref\rangle$$\rightarrow$**size()** > $\langle lowB\rangle$) **and** $\langle TrgContainer\rangle$.**allInstances()** $\rightarrow$**exists**(c | c.$\langle ref\rangle$$\rightarrow$**size()** < $\langle upB\rangle$)]**[1]** [1] add condition if $\langle SrcContainer\rangle$.$\langle ref\rangle$ is not compatible with target type	**Wodel:** **retype one** Activity **as** DataObject **OCL:** Activity.**allInstances()** $\rightarrow$**exists**(a | ConnectingObject.**allInstances()** $\rightarrow$**forAll**(c | (c.to$\rightarrow$**includes**(a) **implies** c.to$\rightarrow$**size()**>0) **and** (c.from$\rightarrow$**includes**(a) **implies** c.from$\rightarrow$**size()**>0))) *-- the checks on references to* *-- and from are performed because* *-- they are not compatible with* *-- DataObjects*
Reference creation: There is an object of the reference type, and a reference to which we can add the object without violating the upper bound.	$\langle TgtClass\rangle$.**allInstances()** $\rightarrow$**exists**(o | $\langle object-filter\rangle$) **and** $\langle SrcClass\rangle$.**allInstances()** $\rightarrow$**exists**(o | $\langle object-filter\rangle$ **and** o.$\langle ref\rangle$$\rightarrow$**size()** < $\langle upB\rangle$)	**Wodel:** **create reference** ^to **to one** Activity **in one** Sequence **OCL:** Activity.**allInstances()**$\rightarrow$**exists**(a | true) **and** Sequence.**allInstances()** $\rightarrow$**exists**(s | s.to$\rightarrow$**size()** < 1)
Reference modification: There is a non-empty reference of the given kind, and more than one object of the reference target type.	$\langle SrcClass\rangle$.**allInstances()** $\rightarrow$**exists**(o | o.$\langle ref\rangle$$\rightarrow$**notEmpty()**) **and** $\langle TgtClass\rangle$.**allInstances()** $\rightarrow$**size()** > 1	**Wodel:** **modify target** ^to **from one** Sequence **to other** FlowObject **OCL:** Sequence.**allInstances()** $\rightarrow$**exists**(s | s.to$\rightarrow$**notEmpty()**) **and** FlowObject.**allInstances()**$\rightarrow$**size()** > 1
Reference deletion: There is a reference from which we can remove an object without violating the lower bound.	$\langle Class\rangle$.**allInstances()** $\rightarrow$**exists**(o | $\langle object-filter\rangle$ **and** o.$\langle ref\rangle$$\rightarrow$**size()** > $\langle lowB\rangle$)	**Wodel:** a = **select one** Sequence **remove** a$\rightarrow$^to **OCL:** Sequence.**allInstances()** $\rightarrow$**exists**(s | s.to$\rightarrow$**size()** > 0)

Overall, the model synthesis process starts with the domain meta-model and its invariants. The meta-model is added an auxiliary mandatory class named Dummy. Then, the process uses the templates of Table 1 to generate the OCL constraints for each mutation operator in the provided WODEL program. These constraints are added as invariants of the Dummy class. Finally, the model finder is invoked with this enriched meta-model as input.

As an example, Listing 3 shows the OCL constraint generated from the program in Listing 1. As the retype operation considers three types, and or with three cases is generated.

```
1  context Dummy
2
3  inv mut1 :
4  StartEv.allInstances()→exists(a | true) or
5  IntermediateEv.allInstances()→exists(a | true) or
6  EndEv.allInstances()→exists(a | true)
```

Listing 3. OCL constraint derived from Listing 1.

Figure 5 shows a seed model returned by the model finder for the previous constraint. It satisfies the constraint of Listing 3, and those of the original meta-model.

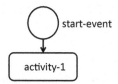

Fig. 5. Generated seed model.

Please note that seed models satisfying the synthesized constraints enable the application of all statements in the WODEL program. However, they do not guarantee that, after applying the program, the resulting mutant satisfies the existing invariants of the domain meta-model. This would require from techniques for advancing constraints to model operations [4], which is left for future work.

5   Tool Support

The WODEL development environment is available as an Eclipse plugin at http://miso.es/tools/Wodel.html, together with examples and videos. The implementation is based on EMF [24], and expects the meta-models of the artefacts to be mutated to be specified using Ecore.

Figure 6 shows the WODEL IDE. The IDE features a textual editor (label 1 in the figure) to create WODEL programs. The editor is built with Xtext and supports features like code completion. Label 2 in the figure shows the explorer with a typical WODEL organization. The src folder contains WODEL programs with the defined mutation operators. These operators are compiled into Java programs, and stored in the src-gen folder. The generated Java programs can be executed within the IDE to produce mutants from the seed models, which are saved in the out folder.

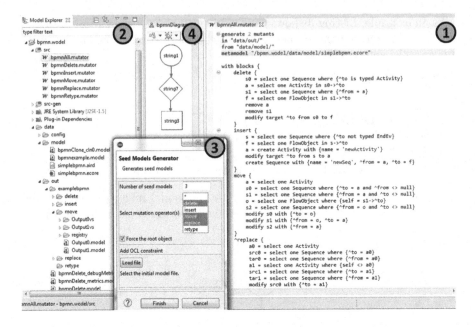

Fig. 6. WODEL IDE and seed model synthesizer.

To support the contributions presented in this paper, we have extended the WODEL environment to support the synthesis of seed models for testing mutation programs. The seed model synthesis for a given program can be configured by means of the wizard marked with label 3 in the figure. This wizard allows setting the maximum number of seed models to be generated, the mutation operators used in the seed model generation process (either all operators in the program or a subset), additional model requirements expressed by OCL, and optionally, an EMF model to be used as seed of the model search. Moreover, a preference page allows customizing the minimum and maximum number of objects and references that the produced seed models should have. The search of seed models is performed using the Use Validator model finder [20]. The generated seed models are converted from the USE format to EMF, and stored in the model folder (see the explorer view). The generated models can be used to test the designed operators, and can be visualized using, e.g., the EMF tree editor, or dedicated graphical editors, such as the one with label 4 in the figure.

6   Related Work

Next, we review works related to the main elements of our approach: languages tailored to define or synthesize mutation operators, and model synthesis from requirements.

DSLs for Mutation Operators, and Operator Synthesis. Some model-based mutation approaches use general-purpose model transformation languages to define mutation operators. In [12], the authors present an MDE approach to define mutation testing tools, where programs are represented as models, and operators are encoded in QVT-o. Mutation operators have also been defined using Henshin in [2], and ATL in [25]. Instead, WODEL is a DSL targeted to define mutation operators, giving support for specific mutation actions (e.g., retyping, cloning), the automatic initialization of object features and containers, and the configuration of the number of mutants to generate. Works like [25] miss such policies and only produce one mutant per input model.

Major [19] is a mutation testing tool for Java that includes a scripting language to perform small customizations in mutation operators. For example, it allows configuring the replacement lists of mutation operators like Arithmetic Operator Replacement (AOR). Instead, WODEL is more expressive as it enables the selection, creation, deletion and retyping of elements. Moreover, WODEL is language-independent, as one can define operators for arbitrary meta-models.

In [1], the authors propose a set of mutation primitives to define mutation operators for Ecore meta-models. However, it is not a full-fledged DSL, missing essential features like the possibility of selecting elements, and there is no tool support for execution. The approach in [2] generates operators that guarantee the consistency of the mutated models with the meta-model multiplicity constraints. The operators are encoded as graph transformation rules. In comparison, WODEL considers more advanced primitives, like cloning, modifying the source or target of references, and retyping. Our techniques for model synthesis (for testing) could be a complement to these two approaches.

Model Synthesis. The MDE community has used model finders (like USE [20] or Alloy [17]) for activities like model completion, test model generation, or transformation analysis. For example, model finding is used in [13] to generate test models for transformations based on specifications. For this purpose, the specifications are transformed into OCL. In our case, the novelty yields in the encoding of the semantics of the WODEL program into OCL, ensuring full statement coverage of the program.

Overall, to the best of our knowledge, environments to support the creation and testing of model-based mutation operators are currently lacking. Hence, we have designed WODEL, and its seed model generation capabilities to fill this gap.

7   Conclusions and Future Work

Given the recurrent need to develop sets of mutation operators, we propose a model-based approach to facilitate their definition, testing, and application. This way, we provide a DSL – called WODEL – for their description, and model synthesis capabilities – based on model finding – for their testing and validation. Our approach is supported by an Eclipse plugin, and we have illustrated the approach in the context of the BPMN language.

We are currently extending the model synthesis process in two ways. First, to generate models where the operators are not applicable but are close to being applicable, so called near misses [23]. Second, to generate seed models ensuring that the execution of the WODEL program leads to a correct model. For this purpose, we may use techniques to advance OCL constraints as preconditions, based on [4]. We also plan to work on static analysis techniques, e.g., to detect operator conflicts and dependencies. Finally, we are currently working on a methodology supporting the integral engineering of mutation operators.

Acknowledgments. Work funded by the Spanish Ministry of Science (projects MASSIVE, RTI2018-095255-B-I00 and FAME, RTI2018-093608-B-C31) and the R&D programme of Madrid (project FORTE, P2018/TCS-4314).

A   BPMN Mutation Operators

Table 2 encodes the BPMN mutation operators proposed in [21] using WODEL.

Table 2. WODEL mutation operators for BPMN.

Mutation operator	Wodel code
Insert activity	s = **select one** Sequence **where** {^to **not typed** EndEv} f = **select one** FlowObject **in** s0→^to a = **create** Activity **with** {name = 'newActivity'} **modify target** ^to **from** s **to** a **create** Sequence **with** {name = 'newSeq', ^from = a, ^to = f}
Remove activity	s0 = **select one** Sequence **where** {^to **is typed** Activity} a = **select one** Activity **in** s0→^to s1 = **select one** Sequence **where** {^from = a} f = **select one** FlowObject **in** s1→^to **remove** a, s1 **modify target** ^to **from** s0 **to** f

Move activity	a = **select one** Activity
	s0 = **select one** Sequence **where** {^to = a **and** ^from <> **null**}
	s1 = **select one** Sequence **where** {^from = a **and** ^to <> **null**}
	o = **select one** FlowObject **where** {**self** = s1→^to}
	s2 = **select one** Sequence **where** {^from = o **and** ^to <> **null**}
	modify s0 **with** {^to = o},
	   s1 **with** {^from = o, ^to = a},
	   s2 **with** {^from = a}

Mutation operator	Wodel code
Replace activity	a0 = **select one** Activity src0 = **select one** Sequence **where** {^to = a0} tar0 = **select one** Sequence **where** {^from = a0} a1 = **select one** Activity **where** {**self** <> a0} src1 = **select one** Sequence **where** {^to = a1} tar1 = **select one** Sequence **where** {^from = a1} **modify** src0 **with** {^to = a1}, tar0 **with** {^from = a1}, src1 **with** {^to = a0}, tar1 **with** {^from = a0}
Retype gateway	**retype one** [AND, OR, XOR] **as** [AND, OR, XOR]

References

1. Alhwikem, F., Paige, R.F., Rose, L., Alexander, R.: A systematic approach for designing mutation operators for MDE languages. In: MODEVA, CEUR Workshop Proceedings, vol. 1713, pp. 54–59 (2016). CEUR-WS.org

2. Burdusel, A., Zschaler, S., John, S.: Automatic generation of atomic consistency preserving search operators for search-based model engineering. In: MODELS, pp. 106–116. IEEE (2019)

3. Cañizares, P.C., Núñez, A., Merayo, M.G.: Mutomvo: mutation testing framework for simulated cloud and HPC environments. J. Syst. Softw. **143**, 187–207 (2018)

4. Cuadrado, J.S., Guerra, E., de Lara, J., Clarisó, R., Cabot, J.: Translating target to source constraints in model-to-model transformations. In: MODELS, pp. 12–22. IEEE Computer Society (2017)

5. DeMillo, R.A., Lipton, R.J., Sayward, F.G.: Hints on test data selection: help for the practicing programmer. IEEE Comput. **11**(4), 34–41 (1978)

6. van Eck, M.L., Buijs, J.C.A.M., van Dongen, B.F.: Genetic process mining: alignment-based process model mutation. In: Fournier, F., Mendling, J. (eds.) BPM 2014. LNBIP, vol. 202, pp. 291–303. Springer, Cham (2015). https://doi.org/10.1007/978-3-319-15895-2_25

7. Estero-Botaro, A., Palomo-Lozano, F., Medina-Bulo, I., Domínguez-Jiménez, J.J., García-Domínguez, A.: Quality metrics for mutation testing with applications to WS-BPEL compositions. Softw. Test. Verif. Reliab. **25**(5–7), 536–571 (2015)

8. Gómez-Abajo, P., Guerra, E., de Lara, J.: Wodel: a domain-specific language for model mutation. In: SAC, pp. 1968–1973. ACM (2016)

9. Gómez-Abajo, P., Guerra, E., de Lara, J.: A domain-specific language for model mutation and its application to the automated generation of exercises. Comput. Lang. Syst. Struct. **49**, 152–173 (2017)

10. Gómez-Abajo, P., Guerra, E., de Lara, J., Merayo, M.G.: A tool for domain-independent model mutation. Sci. Comput. Program. **163**, 85–92 (2018)

11. Gómez-Abajo, P., Guerra, E., de Lara, J., Merayo, M.G.: Mutation testing for DSLs (tool demo). In: DSM, pp. 60–62. ACM (2019)

12. González, A., Luna, C., Bressan, G.: Mutation testing for Java based on model-driven development. In: CLEI-SLISW (2018). (in Spanish)

13. Guerra, E., Soeken, M.: Specification-driven model transformation testing. Softw. Syst. Model. **14**(2), 623–644 (2015)

14. Hamlet, R.G.: Testing programs with the aid of a compiler. IEEE Trans. Software Eng. **3**(4), 279–290 (1977)

15. Harman, M., Jones, B.F.: Search-based software engineering. Inf. Softw. Technol. **43**(14), 833–839 (2001)

16. Herbert, L., Hansen, Z., Jacobsen, P., Cunha, P.: Evolutionary optimization of production materials workflow processes. Procedia CIRP **25**, 53–60 (2014)

17. Jackson, D.: Alloy: a language and tool for exploring software designs. Commun. ACM **62**(9), 66–76 (2019)

18. Jia, Y., Harman, M.: MILU: a customizable, runtime-optimized higher order mutation testing tool for the full C language. In: TAICPART, pp. 94–98 (2008)

19. Just, R.: The major mutation framework: efficient and scalable mutation analysis for Java. In: ISSTA, pp. 433–436. ACM (2014)

20. Kuhlmann, M., Gogolla, M.: From UML and OCL to relational logic and back. In: France, R.B., Kazmeier, J., Breu, R., Atkinson, C. (eds.) MODELS 2012. LNCS, vol. 7590, pp. 415–431. Springer, Heidelberg (2012). https://doi.org/10.1007/978-3-642-33666-9_27

21. Li, C., Reichert, M., Wombacher, A.: On measuring process model similarity based on high-level change operations. In: Li, Q., Spaccapietra, S., Yu, E., Olivé, A. (eds.) ER 2008. LNCS, vol. 5231, pp. 248–264. Springer, Heidelberg (2008). https://doi.org/10.1007/978-3-540-87877-3_19

22. de Medeiros, A., Weijters, A., van der Aalst, W.: Genetic process mining: an experimental evaluation. Data Min. Knowl. Discov. **14**(2), 245–304 (2007)
23. Montaghami, V., Rayside, D.: Bordeaux: a tool for thinking outside the box. In: Huisman, M., Rubin, J. (eds.) FASE 2017. LNCS, vol. 10202, pp. 22–39. Springer, Heidelberg (2017). https://doi.org/10.1007/978-3-662-54494-5_2
24. Steinberg, D., Budinsky, F., Paternostro, M., Merks, E.: EMF: Eclipse Modeling Framework, 2nd edn. Addison-Wesley Professional, Boston (2008)
25. Troya, J., Bergmayr, A., Burgueño, L., Wimmer, M.: Towards systematic mutations for and with ATL model transformations. In: ICST Workshops, pp. 1–10 (2015)
26. Zeller, A., Gopinath, R., Böhme, M., Fraser, G., Holler, C.: Mutation-based fuzzing. In: The Fuzzing Book. Saarland University (2019). https://www.fuzzingbook.org/html/MutationFuzzer.html. Accessed Oct 2019

QBMetrics: A Tool for Evaluating and Comparing Document Schemas

Evandro Miguel Kuszera[1,2]([✉]), Letícia M. Peres[2]([✉]),
and Marcos Didonet Del Fabro[2]([✉])

[1] Federal University of Technology - Paraná, Dois Vizinhos, PR, Brazil
`evandrokuszera@utfpr.edu.br`
[2] C3SL Labs, Federal University of Paraná, Curitiba, PR, Brazil
`{lmperes,marcos.ddf}@inf.ufpr.br`

Abstract. Document stores are frequently used as representation format in many applications. It is often necessary to transform a set of data stored in a relational database (RDB) into a document store. However, it is difficult to evaluate which target document structure is the most appropriate for each scenario. In this article, we present a tool, called QBMetrics (Query-based Metrics), that assists on an RDB to NoSQL document conversion process or even to design a NoSQL database, by calculating a set of query-based metrics for evaluating and comparing the created schemas against a set of existing queries. We represent the schemas and the queries as DAGs (Directed Acyclic Graphs), which are used to calculate the metrics. The metrics allow to evaluate if a given target document schema is adequate to answer the queries. We demonstrate the tool in an RDB to NoSQL conversion scenario, involving the creation of the schemas, queries and the metrics calculation.

Keywords: RDBs · Document stores · Metrics · Evaluation · Tool

1 Introduction

Relational databases (RDB) are widely used to store data of several types of applications. However, they do not meet all requirements imposed by modern applications [9], that handle structured, semi-structured and unstructured data. Furthermore, RDBs are not flexible enough, since they have a predefined schema. NoSQL databases [7] emerged as an option. They differ from RDB in terms of architecture, data model and query language [7]. They are generally classified according to the data model used: document, column family, key-value or graph-based. One of the most used NoSQL format are document stores.

RDB and document stores will be used together, being necessary to investigate strategies to convert and migrate schema and data between them. Different approaches have been presented to convert RDB to NoSQL document stores [1,3,4,8,10]. Some of them consider just the structure of the RDB in the conversion process [8,10]. While others also consider the access pattern of the

© Springer Nature Switzerland AG 2020
N. Herbaut and M. La Rosa (Eds.): CAiSE Forum 2020, LNBIP 386, pp. 77–85, 2020.
https://doi.org/10.1007/978-3-030-58135-0_7

application [1,3,4]. However, none of the approaches is concerned with the evaluation and the comparison of the output document structure against the existing queries that need to be adapted and then executed. The work from [2] presents eleven metrics to evaluate the structure of document stores. Such evaluation is important to guide the choice of an adequate document structure. However, the approach has no specific metrics for assessing the queries access pattern against document structure. Despite not having a formal schema, a document has a structure used by the queries to retrieve data. We consider that this document structure can be used as an abstraction to represent a schema.

We present a demo of the **QBMetrics** tool[1], which is used in RDB to NoSQL document conversion processes or even to design a NoSQL database schema. It provides a graphical interface to calculate query-based metrics that assist on the choice of a most appropriate target NoSQL schema. The tool uses Direct Acyclic Graphs (DAGs) to represent both the target NoSQL schema and the set of queries, where the vertices are entities and the edges are relationships. More specifically, a DAG represent a collection structure for a schema and an access pattern for a query. DAGs as schema have already been used in a previous approach to convert RDB to NoSQL nested models [6].

This demonstration will show how the tool is used to calculate metrics to evaluate and compare candidate target NoSQL schemas, by executing the following steps:

- creation of the target NoSQL schema and queries;
- calculation of a set of schema scores and query scores;
- analysis of the results.

This paper is organized as follows: Sect. 2 presents the architecture of our tool. In Sect. 3 we present a validation scenario and the demonstration steps. Finally, conclusions are provided in Sect. 4.

2   QBMetrics Tool

The QBMetrics tool supports an RDB to NoSQL document conversion process by calculating metrics for evaluating and comparing target NoSQL schema options, prior to the data conversion. The tool has two components, the Converter and Metric components, as shown in Fig. 1.

2.1   Converter Component

This component defines conversion process, encapsulating the input RDB connection properties, the set of target NoSQL schemas and the set of queries. Both, schemas and queries are represented by DAGs (Directed Acyclic Graphs). A DAG is defined as $G = (V, E)$, where the set of vertices V is related with

---

[1] The tool is available for download at: https://github.com/evandrokuszera/nosql-query-based-metrics.

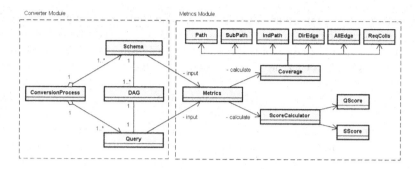

Fig. 1. Tool architecture.

the tables of the RDB and the set of edges E with the relationships between tables. The direction of the edges defines the transformation flow. Each DAG may be seen as a tree, where the root vertex is the target entity. The path from one leaf vertex to the root vertex defines one transformation flow. Each vertex contains the metadata of its respective RDB table, including its name, fields and primary key. The edge between two vertices encapsulates relationship data between two tables, including primary and foreign keys and which entity is on the *one* or *many* side of the relationship. Through the DAG, we specify the de-normalization process from a set of related tables to produce a NoSQL collection. There are works with the same objectives, but with different strategies [3,10].

Considering a DAG as a NoSQL collection, the root vertex is the first level of the collection and the remaining vertices are the nested entities. The direction of the edges defines the direction of nesting between entities and encapsulates nesting type information, including embedded objects or array of embedded objects types. We represent a NoSQL schema through a set of DAGs, where each DAG represents the structure of a collection. We define a NoSQL schema as $S = \{DAG_1, ..., DAG_n | DAG_i \in C\}$, where C is the set of collections of S. The resulting S schema can be used by our Metamoforse framework [6] to migrate data from RDB to NoSQL document

2.2 Metric Component

It receives as input a target NoSQL schema and a set of queries, both represented by DAGs. A detailed description of the metrics is available in [5].

Query Metrics. The tool calculates three metrics that measure the coverage of the query paths in relation to the schema collection paths, being *Path*, *SubPath* and *IndPath*. The *Path(query)* metric measures coverage considering path matching (leaf-to-root vertices), *SubPath(query)* considering subpath matching and *IndPath(query)* considering indirect path matching. An indirect path is the one where all its vertices and edges are contained in a regular path, but there are additional intermediate vertices. The tool also calculates two metrics related to edge coverage. $DirEdge(query)$ measures the coverage of the edges of the query against the edges of the collection, considering the direction of edges (e.g. $a \rightarrow b$). On the other hand, $AllEdge(query)$ measures the edge coverage regardless of edge direction (e.g. $a \rightarrow b$ or $a \leftarrow b$). The last metric is called $ReqColls(query)$, which returns the smallest number of collections required to answer a given query.

To measure the coverage of the query paths and query edges relative to all the schema, the maximum value found when applying the metric for each collection is considered. However, for the $ReqColls$ is minimum value found.

Query Score (QScore) represents the query score for a given metric or set of metrics. The $QScore$ for $DirEdge$, $AllEdge$ and $ReqColls$ is the same value returned by the respective metric, for example, $QScore(DirEdge, query) = DirEdge(query)$. However, for the $Path$, $SubPath$ and $IndPath$ metrics, it is calculated as the maximum value between them and is defined as $QScore(Paths) = max(Path, SubPath, IndPath)$.

To calculate the value of $Path$, $SubPath$ and $IndPath$ in $QScore(Paths)$, we use the expression $(xPath(query) * w)/depth(query)$, where $xPath$ can be replaced for one of the three metrics above, w is the weight of each metric and $depth()$ is a function that returns the depth where the $xPath$ match was found in the schema. Different weights can be assigned to each $xPath$, prioritizing schemas with a specific type of structural correspondence. The match depth is used to penalize schemas, with less deep schemas being preferred.

Schema Score (SScore) denotes the sum of the $QScore$ values for all the queries for a given metric (except $ReqColls$), where each query q_i of the set of queries (Q) has a specific weight w_i, and the sum of all w_i is equal to 1. Following the same idea of the $QScore$, $SScore(Paths, Q)$ denotes the schema score for the metrics $Path$, $SubPath$, and $IndPath$. The $SScore$ for $ReqColls$ metric is a ratio between the number of queries and the number of collections required to answer them. A schema that answers each input query through only one collection has $SScore(ReqColls, Q) = 1$. It decreases when the number of collections increases.

To summarize, the $QScores$ shows the coverage provided by the schema for each query, where we can identify which queries require the most attention or are not covered by the schema. The $SScore$ field provides an overview of how well the schema fits the query set. Since the metrics are not independent, we do not define a single expression to calculate the overall score of the schema.

3   QBMetrics Demonstration

3.1   Scenario

The tool's demonstration scenario consists of converting an existing RDB to NoSQL document. Figure 2 shows the E-R model of the RDB. Although the

RDB is composed of seven tables, related to each other, in the demo only the *Customers, Orders* and *Orderlines* tables will be used. Generally, the RDB entities are converted to documents and the relationships to references, embedded documents or arrays of embedded documents. The decision on how the documents will be structured is not a trivial task and depends on the various aspects (application access pattern, redundancy, maintainability, etc.).

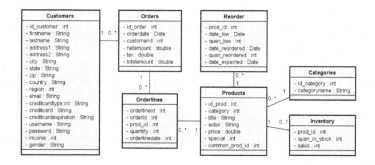

Fig. 2. Input RDB

Figure 3 shows three options for structuring the entities *Customers, Orders* and *Orderlines* as documents, named schemas *A, B* and *C*. In schema *A* we have a collection called *Customers*, where *Orders* and *Orderlines* are arrays of embedded documents. In schema *B* there is a collection called *Orders*, where *Customers* is an embedded document and *Orderlines* is an array of embedded documents. In schema *C* there are two collections, *Customers* and *Orders*.

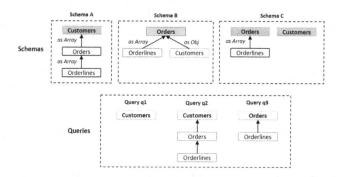

Fig. 3. Input NoSQL document schemas $(A - C)$ and queries $(q_1 - q_3)$.

In this demo, we consider the application access pattern to evaluate and compare the schemas $A - C$. The access pattern is represented by the queries $q_1 - q_3$ of Fig. 3. The goal is to calculate the metrics on the set of schemas and check which one provides greater coverage for the set of queries. The user can configure different weights for queries, prioritizing a certain access pattern. In addition, it is also possible to assign different weights to the *Path, SubPath* and *IndPath* metrics, prioritizing schemas by path type. In the demonstration scenario, all queries will have the same weight (same priority), however, different weights will be assigned for path type, being *path* = 1.0, *subpath* = 0.7 and *indpath* = 0.5. In this way, schemas with greater *Path* coverage will be prioritized, followed by schemas with greater *SubPath* and *IndPath* coverage.

3.2 Demonstration

The tool provides support for defining a conversion process from RDB to NoSQL document, and also for evaluating and comparing possible NoSQL schemas through query-based metrics. Figure 4 shows the graphical interface of the tool. The execution flow is based on four steps: In (A) the input RDB connection parameters are provided. In (B) one or more NoSQL schemas are created from the entities of the input RDB. In (C), queries that represent the application's access pattern are defined. Finally, in (D) the metrics are calculated. Each step will be detailed below.

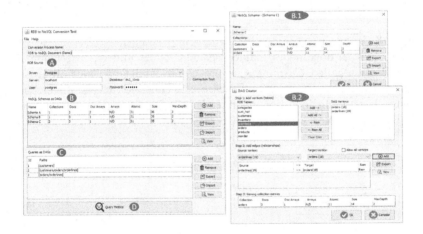

Fig. 4. The tool graphical interface

A: Input RDB. The starting point is to define the connection properties of the input RDB (A). The tool accesses the RDB metadata to assist in creating schemas and queries. Currently, Postgres and MySQL databases are supported.

B: NoSQL Schemas. The user can create one or more NoSQL schemas from the input RDB. Each schema consists of one or more collections of documents, represented as DAGs. In Fig. 4 (B), schemas $A - C$ and respective values for structural metrics are shown, such as number of documents, arrays of embedded documents, arrays of primitive types, primitive types and the maximum collection depth. The user can add new collections or remove existing collections from the schema. In Fig. 4 (B.1) schema C is shown. It is composed of the *Customers* and *Orders* collections. In Fig. 4 (B.2) the screen for creating a collection (or DAG) is shown. To create a collection three steps are required:

- **Step 1 - Add vertices**: the user selects the vertices (RDB tables) to compose the DAG. The tool automatically loads the list of tables from the input RDB. For instance, in (B.2) the *Orders* and *Orderlines* vertices are selected.
- **Step 2 - Add edges**: the user adds edges between vertices. When selecting the source vertex, the tool automatically searches for possibly target vertex, based on RDB metadata. For example, in (B.2) an edge is added in the direction *Orderlines* → *Orders*. The direction of the edges, together with metadata extracted from the input RDB (e.g. PK and FK) define how the entities will be nested. In this case, *Orderlines* (FK) will be nested as an array of documents embedded in the collection *Orders* (PK).
- **Step 3 - Collection metrics**: show the structural metrics of the collection.

The next step is to create the queries, which will be used to calculate the metrics on the NoSQL schemas.

C: Queries. The process of creating queries is similar to the process of creating collections. Both, collections and queries, use DAG-based abstraction. Fig. 4 (C) shows the three previously defined queries (from Fig. 3). These queries represent the access pattern that will be used to evaluate and compare the schemas $A - C$.

D: Calculating Query Metrics. After defining the candidate NoSQL schemas and queries, the user can calculate the metrics. Figure 5 shows the results of the

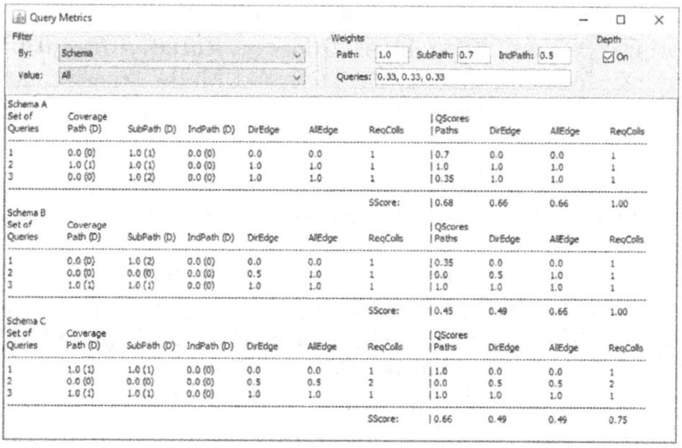

Fig. 5. Query metrics results by schema

metrics for the schemas $A - C$ and queries $q_1 - q_3$, including query coverage (left side), $QScore$ (right side) and $SScore$ (below each schema).

Field (D) represents the depth where the correspondence between schema and query was identified. As a result, among schemas A, B and C, schema A has the highest $SScore$ for the $Paths$ (0.68) and $DirEdge$ (0.66) metrics, being the schema closest to the query access pattern. The schema C is in second place, but has the lowest $SScore$ for the $ReqColls$ (0.75) metric, which means it is necessary to join documents from different collections. Through the metrics, the user can evaluate and compare different NoSQL schema options before migrating the data, where the user can select one or more metrics that best meet the requirements of the application.

4   Conclusion

In this demo paper we presented the **QBMetrics** tool to support the conversion process from RDB to NoSQL document. Based on an input RDB, the expert user defines a set of candidate NoSQL schemas and a set of queries that represent the application's access pattern, both represented as DAGs. The tool calculates a set of metrics that measures the coverage that a schema provides for the set of queries. This information is used to decide which schema is most appropriate for the required access pattern, before migrating the data. As a future work, we intend to extend the set of metrics to consider aspects related to the implementation effort and execution time of queries in the target database. In addition, it is planned to carry out evaluations of the tool in real scenarios.

References

1. Freitas, M.C.d., Souza, D.Y., Salgado, A.C.: Conceptual mappings to convert relational into NoSQL databases. In: Proceedings of the 18th ICEIS (2016)
2. Gómez, P., Roncancio, C., Casallas, R.: Towards Quality Analysis for Document Oriented Bases. In: Trujillo, J.C., et al. (eds.) ER 2018. LNCS, vol. 11157, pp. 200–216. Springer, Cham (2018). https://doi.org/10.1007/978-3-030-00847-5_16
3. Jia, T., Zhao, X., Wang, Z., Gong, D., Ding, G.: Model transformation and data migration from relational database to MongoDB. In: IEEE BigData, pp. 60–67 (2016)
4. Karnitis, G., Arnicans, G.: Migration of relational database to document-oriented database: Structure denormalization and data transformation. In: 2015 7th ICCI-CSN, pp. 113–118 (2015)
5. Kuszera, E.M., Peres, L.M., Didonet Del Fabro, M.: Query-based metrics for evaluating and comparing document schemas. In: Dustdar, S., Yu, E., Salinesi, C., Rieu, D., Pant, V. (eds.) CAiSE 2020. LNCS, vol. 12127, pp. 530–545. Springer, Cham (2020). https://doi.org/10.1007/978-3-030-49435-3_33
6. Kuszera, E.M., Peres, L.M., Fabro, M.D.D.: Toward RDB to NoSQL: transforming data with metamorfose framework. In: Proceedings of the 34th ACM/SIGAPP Symposium on Applied Computing, pp. 456–463. SAC 2019 (2019)
7. Sadalage, P.J., Fowler, M.: NoSQL Distilled: A Brief Guide to the Emerging World of Polyglot Persistence, 1st edn. Addison-Wesley Professional, Boston (2012)

8. Stanescu, L., Brezovan, M., Burdescu, D.D.: Automatic mapping of MySQL databases to NoSQL MongoDB. In: 2016 FedCSIS, pp. 837–840, September 2016
9. Stonebraker, M., Madden, S., Abadi, D.J., Harizopoulos, S., Hachem, N., Helland, P.: The end of an architectural era (it's time for a complete rewrite). In: Proceedings of 33rd VLDB, University of Vienna, Austria, 23–27 September 2007, pp. 1150–1160 (2007)
10. Zhao, G., Lin, Q., Li, L., Li, Z.: Schema conversion model of SQL database to NoSQL. In: 2014 Ninth 3PGCIC, pp. 355–362 (2014)

Probabilistic Conformance Checking Based on Declarative Process Models

Fabrizio Maria Maggi[1(✉)], Marco Montali[1], and Rafael Peñaloza[2]

[1] Free University of Bozen-Bolzano, Bolzano, Italy
{maggi,montali}@inf.unibz.it
[2] University of Milano-Bicocca, Milan, Italy
rafael.penaloza@unimib.it

Abstract. Conformance checking is a fundamental task to detect deviations between the actual and the expected courses of execution of a business process. In this context, temporal business constraints have been extensively adopted to declaratively capture the expected behavior of the process. However, traditionally, these constraints are interpreted logically in a crisp way: a process execution trace conforms with a constraint model if all the constraints therein are satisfied. This is too restrictive when one wants to capture best practices, constraints involving uncontrollable activities, and exceptional but still conforming behaviors. This calls for the extension of business constraints with uncertainty. In this paper, we tackle this timely and important challenge, relying on recent results on probabilistic temporal logics over finite traces. Specifically, we equip business constraints with a natural, probabilistic notion of uncertainty. We discuss the semantic implications of the resulting framework and show how probabilistic conformance checking and constraint entailment can be tackled therein.

Keywords: Declarative process models · Probabilistic temporal logics · Conformance checking

1 Introduction

Temporal business constraints have been extensively adopted to declaratively capture the acceptable courses of execution of a business process for conformance checking. In particular, the *Declare* constraint-based process modeling language [8] has been introduced as a front-end language to specify business constraints based on Linear Temporal Logic over finite traces (LTL_f) [2].

In general, business constraints are interpreted logically in a crisp way. This means that an execution trace conforms with a constraint model if all the constraints therein are satisfied. This is too restrictive when one wants to capture patterns that recur in many application domains, such as:

© Springer Nature Switzerland AG 2020
N. Herbaut and M. La Rosa (Eds.): CAiSE Forum 2020, LNBIP 386, pp. 86–99, 2020.
https://doi.org/10.1007/978-3-030-58135-0_8

- best practices, captured as constraints that should hold in the majority, but not necessary all cases (example: an order is shipped via truck in 90% of the cases);
- outlier behaviors, i.e., constraints that only apply to very few cases that should still considered to be conforming (example: an order is shipped via car in less than 1% of the cases);
- constraints involving activities that are not all necessarily controlled by the organization that orchestrates the process, and for which only some guarantees can be given about their proper executability (example: whenever an order is accepted, payment is performed by the customer in 8 cases out of 10).

Surprisingly enough, to the best of our knowledge no attempt has been done, so far, to make constraint-based process modeling approaches able to capture this form of uncertainty. In this paper, we tackle this timely and important challenge, relying on recent results on probabilistic temporal logics over finite traces [5]. Specifically, *we equip business constraints with a natural, probabilistic notion of uncertainty based on the ratio of traces in a log that must satisfy the constraint*, and use the resulting probabilistic constraints to lift Declare to its probabilistic variant that we call ProbDeclare. We then discuss the semantic implications of this approach, showing how it has to combine logical and probabilistic reasoning to tackle the semantics of probabilistic constraints and their interplay. We finally show how this combined reasoning can be applied to verify the consistency of a ProbDeclare model, do conformance checking, and carry out probabilistic constraint entailment, i.e., estimate with which probability a ProbDeclare model implies a given LTL_f formula.

2   LTL over Finite Traces and the Declare Framework

As a formal basis for specifying crisp (temporal) business constraints, we adopt the customary choice of Linear Temporal Logic over finite traces (LTL_f [1,2]). This logic is at the basis of the well-known Declare [8] constraint-based process modeling language. We provide here a gentle introduction to this logic and to the Declare framework.

2.1   Linear Temporal Logic over Finite Traces

LTL_f has exactly the same syntax as standard LTL, but, differently from LTL, it interprets formulae over an unbounded, yet finite linear sequence of states. Given an alphabet Σ of atomic propositions (in our setting, representing activities), an LTL_f formula φ is built by extending propositional logic with temporal operators:

$$\varphi ::= a \mid \neg\varphi \mid \varphi_1 \vee \varphi_2 \mid \bigcirc\varphi \mid \varphi_1 \, \mathcal{U} \, \varphi_2 \quad \text{where } a \in \Sigma.$$

The semantics of LTL_f is given in terms of *finite traces* denoting finite, *possibly empty* sequences $\tau = \langle \tau_0, \ldots, \tau_n \rangle$ of elements of 2^Σ, containing all possible

Table 1. Some Declare templates, their textual and graphical representation, the corresponding LTL$_f$ formalization and the LTL$_f$ formula capturing their complement (i.e., their logical negation).

TEXT	NOTATION	LTL$_f$ FORMULA (φ)	COMPLEMENT ($\neg\varphi$)
existence (a)	1..* $\boxed{a}$	$\Diamond a$	$\Box\neg a$
absence2 (a)	0..1 $\boxed{a}$	$\neg\Diamond(a \wedge \bigcirc\Diamond a)$	$\Diamond(a \wedge \bigcirc\Diamond a)$
response (a, b)	$\boxed{a}\!\!\longrightarrow\!\!\boxed{b}$	$\Box(a \rightarrow \Diamond b)$	$\Diamond(a \wedge \Box\neg b)$
precedence (a, b)	$\boxed{a}\!\!\longrightarrow\!\!\boxed{b}$	$\neg b \mathcal{W} a$	$\neg a \mathcal{U} b$
not-coexistence (a, a)	$\boxed{a}\!\!-\!\!\!\parallel\!\!-\!\!\boxed{b}$	$\neg(\Diamond a \wedge \Diamond b)$	$\Diamond a \wedge \Diamond b$

propositional interpretations of the propositional symbols in Σ. In the context of this paper, consistently with the literature on business process execution traces, we make the simplifying assumption that in each point of the sequence, one and only one element from Σ holds. Under this assumption, τ becomes a total sequence of activity occurrences from Σ, matching the standard notion of (process) execution trace. We indicate with Σ^* the set of all traces over Σ. The evaluation of a formula is done in a given state (i.e., position) of the trace, and we use the notation $\tau, i \models \varphi$ to express that φ holds in the position i of τ. We also use $\tau \models \varphi$ as a shortcut notation for $\tau, 0 \models \varphi$. This denotes that φ holds over the entire trace τ starting from the very beginning and, consequently, logically captures the notion of *conformance* of τ against φ. We also say that φ is *satisfiable* if it admits at least one conforming trace.

In the syntax above, operator $\bigcirc$ denotes the *next state* operator, and $\bigcirc\varphi$ is true if there exists a next state (i.e., the current state is not at the end of the trace), and in the next state φ holds. Operator $\mathcal{U}$ instead is the *until* operator, and $\varphi_1 \mathcal{U} \varphi_2$ is true if φ_1 holds now and continues to hold until eventually, in a future state, φ_2 holds. From these operators, we can derive the usual boolean operators $\wedge$ and $\rightarrow$, the two formulae *true* and *false*, as well as additional temporal operators. We consider, in particular, the following three:

- (eventually) $\Diamond\varphi = true \, \mathcal{U} \, \varphi$ is true if there is a future state where φ holds;
- (globally) $\Box\varphi = \neg\Diamond\neg\varphi$ is true if now and in all future states φ holds;
- (weak until) $\varphi_1 \mathcal{W} \varphi_2 = \varphi_1 \mathcal{U} \varphi_2 \vee \Box\varphi_1$ relaxes the until operator by admitting the possibility that φ_2 never becomes true, in this case by requiring that φ_1 holds now and in all future states.

Example 1. The LTL$_f$ formula $\Box(\text{accept} \rightarrow \Diamond\text{pay})$ models that, whenever an order is accepted, then it is eventually paid. The structure of the formula follows what is called *response template* in Declare.   ◁

2.2 Declare

Declare [8] is a declarative process modeling language based on LTL_f. More specifically, a Declare model fixes a set of activities, and a set of constraints over such activities, formalized using LTL_f formulae. The overall model is then formalized as the conjunction of the LTL_f formulae of its constraints.

Among all possible LTL_f formulae, Declare selects some pre-defined patterns. Each pattern is represented as a Declare template, i.e., a formula with placeholders to be substituted by concrete activities to obtain a constraint. Constraints and templates have a graphical representation; Table 1 lists the Declare templates used in this paper. A Declare model is then graphically represented by showing its activities, and the application of templates to such activities (which indicates how the template placeholders have to be substituted to obtain the corresponding constraint).

Example 2. Consider the following Declare model, constituting a (failed) attempt of capturing a fragment of an order-to-shipment process:

The model indicates that there are two activities to accept or reject an order, that these two activities are mutually exclusive, and that both of them have to be executed. These constraints are obviously contradictory and, in fact, the model is inconsistent, since its LTL_f formula $\Diamond$accept $\wedge$ $\Diamond$reject $\wedge$ $\neg(\Diamond$accept $\wedge$ $\Diamond$reject$)$ is unsatisfiable.   ◁

3 Probabilistic Business Constraints

As recalled in Sect. 2, business constraints captured with LTL_f are interpreted in a crisp way, i.e., they are expected to hold in *every* execution of the process. We now extend constraints with a natural notion of uncertainty introducing probabilistic constraints. Then, we show how this notion can be used to make Declare probabilistic and discuss informally the interplay of multiple probabilistic constraints.

3.1 Probabilistic Constraints: Definition and Semantics

For simplicity, we only consider the case of *exact* probability, but all the considerations we do directly carry over the more general case where the probability of a constraint is related to a given quantity with comparison operators ($\leq$, $<$, $=$, and their duals).

Definition 1. *A probabilistic constraint over a set Σ of activities is a pair $\langle\varphi, p\rangle$, where φ is an LTL_f formula over Σ representing the constraint formula, and p is a rational value in $[0, 1]$ representing the constraint probability.*   ◁

Since a probabilistic constraint quantifies *how many* traces should satisfy it, it has to be interpreted over multiple traces that, as a whole, constitute an event log for the process of interest. In particular, the *constraint holds in a log if the ratio of traces in the log that satisfy the constraint formula is equal to the constraint probability*. This naturally leads to interpret the constraint probability statistically as the ratio of conforming vs non-conforming traces contained in a given log.

For simplicity, we stick here with the standard definition of event log, but we could alternatively adopt the stochastic interpretation of an event log, following [3].

Definition 2. *An* (event) log *over a set Σ of activities is a multiset of traces over Σ, i.e., a multiset over Σ^*.*   ◁

Given a log $\mathcal{L}$, we write $\tau^n \in \log$ to indicate that trace τ appears n times in $\mathcal{L}$. Trace τ belongs to $\mathcal{L}$ if $\tau^n \in \log$ with $n > 0$. With these notions at hand, we say that a probabilistic constraint $\langle \varphi, p \rangle$ holds in a log $\mathcal{L}$ or, equivalently, that $\mathcal{L}$ satisfies $\langle \varphi, p \rangle$, if $\sum_{\tau^n \in \mathcal{L}, \tau \models \varphi} n = p$.

Note that the probabilistic constraint $\langle \varphi, p \rangle$ is equivalent to the probabilistic constraint $\langle \neg\varphi, 1 - p \rangle$. In fact, given a log $\mathcal{L}$, if the ratio of traces in $\mathcal{L}$ that satisfies φ is p, then the remaining $1 - p$ traces in $\mathcal{L}$ do not satisfy φ, i.e., they satisfy the constraint complement $\neg\varphi$.

Example 3. Consider the probabilistic constraint $\langle \text{existence}(\text{accept}), 0.8 \rangle$. It indicates that 80% of the traces in a log contain at least one occurrence of accept or, equivalently, that 20% of the traces do not contain any execution of accept. This constraint holds in the log: $\left[\langle \text{accept} \rangle^2, \langle \text{accept}, \text{reject} \rangle, \langle \text{reject} \rangle^4, \langle \text{accept}, \text{cancel} \rangle^3, \langle \text{accept}, \text{pay}, \text{ship} \rangle^{10} \right]$, since 16 out of the 20 traces contained therein include (at least) one occurrence of accept, i.e., they satisfy $\text{existence} = \Diamond\text{accept}$.   ◁

3.2   ProbDeclare and the Issue of Multiple Interacting Constraints

We now use the notion of probabilistic constraint as the basic building block to lift Declare to its probabilistic version, which we call ProbDeclare.

Definition 3. *A ProbDeclare model is a pair $\langle \Sigma, \mathcal{C} \rangle$, where Σ is a set of activities and $\mathcal{C}$ is a set of probabilistic constraints.*   ◁

A standard Declare model corresponds to a ProbDeclare model where all probabilistic constraints have probability 1. In the remainder of the paper, when drawing ProbDeclare diagrams, we then adopt the following notation: *(i)* whenever a constraint has probability 1, we draw it as a standard Declare constraint; *(ii)* Whenever a constraint has probability $p < 1$, we show it in light blue, and we annotate it with the probability value p.

The main issue that arises when multiple, genuinely probabilistic constraints are present in the same ProbDeclare model is that they interact with each other depending on their constraint formulae and probabilities. In particular, to satisfy the probabilistic constraints contained in a ProbDeclare model, a log must contain suitable fractions of traces so as to satisfy *all* probabilistic constraints and their probabilities, with the effect that some of these traces may contribute to the computation of the ratios for different constraints. The following examples intuitively illustrate this interplay. The first example shows that inconsistent Declare models may become consistent if the conflicting constraints are associated with suitable probabilities.

Example 4. Consider the following probabilistic variant of the (inconsistent) Declare diagram shown in Example 2.

This model contains two mutually exclusive activities, accept and reject, and indicates that often (in 80% of the cases) accept is selected, whereas rarely (in 10% of the cases) reject is selected. This captures a form of probabilistic choice, which also implicitly contemplates that none of the two activities occurs. In fact, from this very simple model, we can infer the following conditions on satisfying logs:

1. The not-coexistence constraint linking accept and reject is crisp, and consequently no trace in the log can contain both accept and reject.
2. Point 1, combined with the probabilistic existence constraint on accept, means that a trace in the log has 0.8 probability of containing accept (which means that reject will not occur), and 0.2 probability of not containing accept (which means that reject may occur or not).
3. A similar line of reasoning can be applied to the existence of reject, which must appear in 10% of the traces in the log.

All in all, combining all the constraints, we get that the 10% of traces containing reject must be disjoint from the 80% containing accept. This implicitly means that in the remaining 10% of the traces, none of the two activities occur.   ◁

The second example shows that a consistent ProbDeclare model may become inconsistent by changing the values of probabilities.

Example 5. Consider again the ProbDeclare diagram in Example 4. Clearly, if we change to 1 the constraint probabilities attached to the two existence constraints, the model becomes identical to that in Example 2, consequently becoming inconsistent. More in general, the model becomes inconsistent whenever the sum of the two probabilities exceeds 1. This witnesses that there must exist some traces in which both constraints are satisfied, which contradicts the fact that accept and reject should not coexist. More precisely, if we denote by p_a and p_r the probabilities attached to the two existence constraints, then there is a probability $p_a + p_r - 1$ of having a trace that contains both accept and reject. For example, if we set $p_a = 0.8$ and $p_r = 0.3$, we have that 10% of the traces in the log should contain both accept and reject, which is impossible given the fact that every trace in the log should satisfy not-coexistence(accept, reject).   ◁

The last example shows that, as customary in models with uncertainty, it is misleading to just consider the probabilities attached to single constraints when one wants to assess the probability of satisfying all of them at once.

Example 6. Consider the following ProbDeclare model:

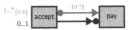

The model indicates that an order can be accepted at most once, and that often (in 80% of the cases) it is actually accepted. In addition, it captures that with probability 0.7 it is true that, whenever the order is accepted, then it is also consequently paid (multiple payment instalments are possible, by simply repeating the execution of pay). Finally, payments are enabled only if the order has been previously accepted.

By looking at the diagram, one could wrongly interpret that in 70% of the cases it is true that the order is accepted and then paid. This is wrong because the response(accept, pay) constraint can also be (vacuously) satisfied by a trace that does not contain at all occurrences of accept. A natural question is then: what is the actual probability of observing traces that at some point contain accept and, later on, pay (possibly with other activity occurrences in between and afterward)? The answer is that this happens in half of the cases. To justify this non-trivial answer, one has to apply combined reasoning by considering the interplay of response(accept, pay) and existence(accept), with their corresponding probabilities. More specifically, response(accept, pay) can be satisfied in this model in two different ways:

1. by not executing at all accept;
2. by executing accept (which can be done only once, due to the presence of the crisp absence2(accept) constraint) and, later on, at least once pay.

These two situations, which we will call later on *constraint scenarios*, should altogether cover exactly 70% of the traces, as dictated by the constraint probability attached to response(accept, pay). The first scenario must have probability 0.2, because in 80% of the traces accept must appear, as dictated by the existence(accept) constraint and its associated probability. But then, the second scenario, which is the one we are interested in, has probability $0.7 - 0.2 = 0.5$ (half of the traces in the log). ◁

In the next section, we make the reasoning carried out in the discussed examples more systematic, showing how logical and probabilistic reasoning have to be combined towards a single, combined declarative framework.

4   Reasoning on Time and Probabilities

As we have seen in the previous section, to reason on conjunctions of probabilistic constraints, i.e., on ProbDeclare models, we need to simultaneously take into account the temporal semantics of constraints and their associated probabilities.

Formally, this is done by relying on the probabilistic temporal logic over finite traces PLTL_f, recently introduced in [5]. More specifically, probabilistic constraints as defined here have a direct encoding into the fragment PLTL_f^0 of PLTL_f, also investigated in [5]. We do not delve into the encoding, nor highlight the formal details on how to carry out this combined reasoning. We instead show algorithmically how to accomplish this, noticing that all the algorithmic techniques discussed next are correct thanks to [5]. Again thanks to [5], we also get that, overall, the cost of reasoning on probabilistic constraints has the same complexity of reasoning with standard LTL_f constraints, i.e., PSPACE in the length of the constraints (this complexity bound is tight).

In the remainder of this section, we fix a ProbDeclare model $\mathcal{M} = \langle \Sigma, \mathcal{C} \rangle$, where $\mathcal{C}$ is partitioned into *crisp constraints* $\mathcal{C}_{crisp} = \{\langle \varphi, p \rangle \in \mathcal{C} \mid p = 1\}$ and (genuinely) *probabilistic constraints* $\mathcal{C}_{prob} = \{\langle \varphi, p \rangle \in \mathcal{C} \mid p < 1\}$. With a slight abuse of terminology, when we use the term "crisp constraint", we mean a constraint in $\mathcal{C}_{crisp}$, and, when we use the term "probabilistic constraint", we mean a constraint in $\mathcal{C}_{prob}$. We also assume that $\mathcal{C}_{crisp}$ is a consistent Declare model, i.e., crisp constraints are satisfiable altogether. If not, then $\mathcal{M}$ has to be discarded, as it does not admit any conforming trace.

4.1 Constraint Scenarios and Consistency of ProbDeclare Models

While crisp constraints must hold in every possible trace, probabilistic constraints may or may not hold (with a ratio specified by their probability). In addition, recall that when a constraint formula does not hold, then its negation must hold. Consequently, in the most general case, $\mathcal{M}$ is a compact description for the $2^{|\mathcal{C}_{prob}|}$ standard Declare models, each one obtained by considering all constraint formulae in $\mathcal{C}_{crisp}$, and by selecting, for each constraint $\langle \varphi, p \rangle \in \mathcal{C}_{prob}$, whether the constraint formula φ or its complement $\neg\varphi$ is assumed to hold.

We call the so-obtained Declare models *(constraint) scenarios*. To pinpoint a specific scenario, we fix an ordering over $\mathcal{C}_{prob}$, and we denote the scenario with a binary string of length $|\mathcal{C}_{prob}|$, where position number $i \in \{1, \ldots, |\mathcal{C}_{prob}|\}$ has value 1 if the i-th probabilistic constraint in $\mathcal{C}_{prob}$ must hold, 0 otherwise.

Example 7. Consider the ProbDeclare model in Example 6. By fixing the ordering over its probabilistic constraints where $\langle \texttt{existence}(\textsf{accept}), 0.8 \rangle$ is first and $\langle \texttt{response}(\textsf{accept}, \textsf{pay}), 0.7 \rangle$ is second, we have the following 4 scenarios:

1. Scenario 00, where none of the two constraint formulae holds, and is consequently characterized by formula $\square\neg\textsf{accept} \wedge \Diamond(\textsf{accept} \wedge \square\neg\textsf{pay})$.
2. Scenario 01, where the **response** constraint formula holds while the **existence** one does not, and so has formula $\square\neg\textsf{accept} \wedge \square(\textsf{accept} \rightarrow \Diamond\textsf{pay})$.
3. Scenario 10, where the **existence** constraint formula holds while the **response** one does not, and so has formula $\Diamond\textsf{accept} \wedge \Diamond(\textsf{accept} \wedge \square\neg\textsf{pay})$.
4. Scenario 11, where both formulae holds ($\Diamond\textsf{accept} \wedge \square(\textsf{accept} \rightarrow \Diamond\textsf{pay})$). ◁

Among the possible scenarios, only those that are logically consistent, i.e., are associated with a satisfiable formula, have to be retained. In fact, inconsistent scenarios do not admit any conforming trace. Obviously, when checking whether the scenario is consistent, its constraint formulae have to be conjoined with those in $\mathcal{C}_{crisp}$.

Example 8. Consider the 4 scenarios of Example 7. Scenario 00 has to be discarded because it is logically inconsistent: its formula $\Box\neg$accept $\wedge \Diamond$(accept $\wedge$ $\Diamond$pay) is unsatisfiable (it is asking for the presence and absence of accept). The other three scenarios are instead logically consistent.   ◁

Example 9. Consider the ProbDeclare model in Example 4. Also for this model there are 4 scenarios, obtained by considering the two existence constraints and their complements. The scenario where both constraints are not satisfied captures those traces where no decision is taken for the order, i.e., the order is not accepted nor rejected. The scenarios where one constraint is satisfied and the other is not account for those traces where a univocal decision is taken for the order. The scenario where both constraints are satisfied, thus requiring acceptance and rejection for the order, is inconsistent, due to the interplay of such constraints and the crisp not-coexistence one. This corresponds to the standard Declare model of Example 2.   ◁

We have explicitly used the term *logically* (in)consistent scenarios since there is no guarantee that these scenarios are actually plausible. This depends on their corresponding probabilities, which, in turn, are obtained by suitably combining the probabilities of their constitutive constraints in their positive or complemented form. This is done by enforcing the semantics of constraint probability, which requires to ensure the following: for every probabilistic constraint $\langle \varphi, p \rangle$, the sum of the probabilities assigned to those scenarios where φ must hold must be equal to p.

To do so, we construct a system of linear inequalities whose variables represent the probabilities of possible scenarios [5]. We denote such variables as x_s, where s is the boolean string representing the scenario the variable is associated with. By considering a ProbDeclare model $\mathcal{M}$, fixing $n = |\mathcal{C}_{prob}|$ and writing $i \in \{0, \ldots, n-1\}$ in binary, the system of inequalities $\mathcal{L}_{\mathcal{M}}$ is:

$$x_i \geq 0 \qquad 0 \leq i < 2^n \qquad (x_i \text{ are probabilities})$$

$$\sum_{i=0}^{2^n-1} x_i = 1 \qquad\qquad\qquad (x_i \text{ are probabilities})$$

$$\sum_{j\text{th position is }1} x_i = p_j \qquad 0 \leq j < n \qquad (\text{constraint semantics})$$

$$x_i = 0 \qquad\qquad \text{if scenario } i \text{ is logically inconsistent}$$

Notably, $\mathcal{L}_{\mathcal{M}}$ combines, at once, the logical and the probabilistic content of $\mathcal{M}$, on the one hand, imposing that the scenario probabilities agree with the constraint probabilities, and, on the other, forcing logically inconsistent scenario to have probability 0.

$\mathcal{L}_\mathcal{M}$ may admit: *(i) no solution*, witnessing that $\mathcal{M}$ is inconsistent; *(ii) one solution*, returning the exact probabilities for all the scenarios of $\mathcal{M}$, *(iii) multiple (possibly infinitely many) solutions*, witnessing that different probability distributions can be assigned to the scenarios. To obtain the ranges of probability for each scenario, one can turn the system of inequality into several optimizations problems where each probability variable is minimized and maximized.

It is worth noting that, when $\mathcal{L}_\mathcal{M}$ is solvable, its solutions may force some scenario probabilities to be always equal to 0. This witnesses the fact that even a logically consistent scenario may not have any conforming trace due to the interplay of constraint probabilities. We call *plausible* those scenarios that have a probability > 0.

Example 10. Consider again the ProbDeclare model in Example 7 with its 4 scenarios (one of which is logically inconsistent, as discussed in Example 8). The four possible scenarios have corresponding probability variables x_{00}, x_{01}, x_{10} and x_{11}, constrained by the system of inequalities (we omit the fact that all variables are non-negative):

$$x_{00} + x_{01} + x_{10} + x_{11} = 1$$
$$x_{10} + x_{11} = 0.8 \qquad \text{semantics of } \langle \texttt{existence}(\texttt{accept}), 0.8 \rangle$$
$$x_{01} \phantom{{}+{}} + x_{11} = 0.7 \qquad \text{semantics of } \langle \texttt{response}(\texttt{accept}, \texttt{pay}), 0.7 \rangle$$
$$x_{00} \phantom{{}+ x_{11}} = 0 \qquad \text{logical inconsistency of scenario 00}$$

The system admits a single solution, with $x_{00} = 0$, $x_{01} = 0.2$, $x_{10} = 0.3$ and $x_{11} = 0.5$, the last matching the informal discussion given in Example 6. ◁

We conclude the section with an informative ProbDeclare model example that combines parts of the examples seen so far to capture a non-trivial fragment of an order-to-shipment process. We use parameters for constraint probabilities, then discussing the impact of grounding such probabilities to different actual values.

Example 11. Consider the following order-to-shipment ProbDeclare model:

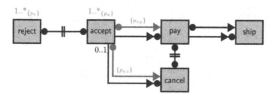

To construct the 16 possible scenarios for this model, the following constraints and LTL$_f$ formulae have to be considered:

- `existence(accept)` with formula $\varphi_a = \Diamond \texttt{accept}$, and its complement $\Box \neg \texttt{accept}$;
- `existence(reject)` with formula $\varphi_r = \Diamond \texttt{reject}$, and its complement $\Box \neg \texttt{reject}$;
- `response(accept, pay)` with formula $\varphi_{ap} = \Box(\texttt{accept} \rightarrow \Diamond \texttt{pay})$, and its complement $\Diamond(\texttt{accept} \wedge \Box \neg \texttt{pay})$;

- response(accept, cancel) with formula $\varphi_{ax} = \Box(\text{accept} \rightarrow \Diamond\text{cancel})$, and its complement $\Diamond(\text{accept} \wedge \Box\neg\text{cancel})$. ◁

Table 2 summarizes the different constraint scenarios, their logical consistency and, in the last column, their probabilities computed by constructing and solving the system of inequalities described above. Table 3 shows instead three different groundings for the constraint probability parameters and their impact on the probabilities of the scenarios. In particular, *Case 1* is so that all the logically consistent scenarios may actually occur, even though with different probabilities. The most likely scenario, accounting for half of the traces, captures the happy path where the order is paid and shipped. *Case 2* assigns a different probability to response(accept, cancel), causing scenario 1000 to be not plausible anymore, being associated with probability 0; intuitively, the interplay of constraints and their probabilities makes it impossible to just execute accept without taking further activities. Finally, *Case 3* increases the probability of response(accept, cancel) even more, resulting in an inconsistent model.

Table 2. Constraint scenarios of the ProbDeclare model in Example 11, indicating whether they are logically consistent and, if so, providing the (shortest) conforming trace, and the scenario probability.

Scenario				Logically consistent	Shortest conforming trace	Scenario probability
φ_a	φ_r	φ_{ap}	φ_{ax}			
0	0	0	0	N		
0	0	0	1	N		
0	0	1	0	N		
0	0	1	1	Y	Empty trace	$1 - p_a - p_r$
0	1	0	0	N		
0	1	0	1	N		
0	1	1	0	N		
0	1	1	1	Y	⟨reject⟩	p_r
1	0	0	0	Y	⟨accept⟩	$2 - p_a - p_{ap} - p_{ax}$
1	0	0	1	Y	⟨accept, cancel⟩	$p_a + p_{ax} - 1$
1	0	1	0	Y	⟨accept, pay, ship⟩	$p_a + p_{ap} - 1$
1	0	1	1	N		
1	1	0	0	N		
1	1	0	1	N		
1	1	1	0	N		
1	1	1	1	N		

Table 3. Three different groundings for the constraint probabilities used in the Prob-Declare model in Example 11, and their impact on the scenario probabilities.

Consistent scenario				Case 1	Case 2	Case 3
φ_a	φ_r	φ_{ap}	φ_{ax}	$p_a = 0.8$	$p_a = 0.8$	$p_a = 0.8$
				$p_r = 0.1$	$p_r = 0.1$	$p_r = 0.1$
				$p_{ap} = 0.7$	$p_{ap} = 0.7$	$p_{ap} = 0.7$
				$p_{ax} = 0.3$	$p_{ax} = 0.5$	$p_{ax} = 0.7$
0	0	1	1	0.1	0.1	Inconsistent
0	1	1	1	0.1	0.1	
1	0	0	0	0.2	0	
1	0	0	1	0.1	0.3	
1	0	1	0	0.5	0.5	

5   Reasoning with Constraint Scenarios

Constraint scenarios can be used to perform a variety of tasks. We focus here on two fundamental ones: conformance checking and probabilistic constraint entailment.

5.1   Conformance Checking

In Declare, the simplest form of conformance checking amounts to check whether a given execution trace satisfies all constraints contained in the model, thus returning a yes/no answer.

In ProbDeclare, this notion can be refined by considering the different constraint scenarios and their probabilities. Let $\mathcal{M} = \langle \Sigma, \mathcal{C} \rangle$ be a ProbDeclare model, and τ be a trace over Σ. The plausible scenarios of $\mathcal{M}$ are pairwise disjoint subsets of the overall set Σ^* of traces over Σ. Disjointness comes from the fact that every pair of plausible scenarios is so that they disagree about at least one constraint, and no trace can conform with both of them. The complement of the traces accepted by the plausible scenarios then characterizes those traces that are not conforming with $\mathcal{M}$. To assess conformance, we can then proceed as follows: (1) Check τ against every plausible scenario of $\mathcal{M}$. (2) If one plausible scenario is so that τ holds there, output *yes* together with the probability (or range of probabilities) attached to that scenario; the scenario probability gives an indication on whether the trace represents a "mainstream" execution of the process, or is instead an outlier behavior. (3) If no such scenario is found, then output *no*.

Example 12. Consider the ProbDeclare model captured by *Case 1* in Table 3. Trace $\langle \mathsf{accept}, \mathsf{cancel}, \mathsf{pay} \rangle$ does not conform with the model, since paying and canceling are mutually exclusive. Trace $\langle \mathsf{accept}, \mathsf{cancel} \rangle$ is instead conforming, as it satisfies scenario 1001. Since this scenario is associated with probability 0.1, the analyzed trace represents an outlier behavior. Finally, trace

⟨accept, pay, ship, ship, pay, ship⟩ represents a mainstream behavior since it conforms with the most likely scenario 1010, with probability 0.5.   ◁

5.2   Constraint Entailment

It is well-known that Declare and other declarative process modeling languages have the issue of *hidden dependencies* [7], namely the fact that constraints may interact with each other in subtle ways. This becomes even more complex in the case of probabilistic constraints. In this light, it becomes crucial to be able to ascertain whether a constraint is implied by a given model. Checking constraint implication in Declare is very simple: this simply amounts to check whether the LTL$_f$ formula of the model implies the given constraint. In the case of ProbDeclare, we extend this approach by computing, for a given LTL$_f$ formula, what is the probability with which it is implied by the ProbDeclare model. This is done as follows: (1) Initialize the constraint probability range to 0, 0. (2) For every plausible scenario, check whether the scenario implies the formula of interest in the classical LTL$_f$ sense; if so, update the constraint probability by summing its minimum and maximum to the minimum and maximum probability associated with the scenario. (3) Return the constraint probability range.

Example 13. Consider again the ProbDeclare model captured by *Case 1* in Table 3. We want to check to what extent the model implies that the order is eventually shipped (◇ship). Shipment only occur if a payment occurs before, and therefore this formula is implied only by scenario 1010, consequently getting a probability of 0.5.

We are also interested in checking to what extent the model implies that the order is not rejected (¬◇reject). This formula holds in all those scenarios where existence(reject) is false. Therefore, this formula is implied with probability 0.9.

Finally, consider the LTL$_f$ constraint ¬(◇cancel ∧ ◇ship), expressing the mutual exclusion between cancel and ship. This constraint is implied with probability 1, due to the presence of the two crisp constraints not-coexistence(cancel, pay) and precedence(pay, ship), which must hold in every possible scenario (including the plausible ones).   ◁

6   Conclusions

We have studied how to enrich constraint-based process models with uncertainty, captured as the probability that a trace will conform with a constraint or not. We have discussed how this impacts the semantics of a constraint model, and how logical and probabilistic reasoning have to be combined to provide core services such as consistency and conformance checking, as well as probabilistic constraint entailment.

Notably, all the techniques presented in this paper can be directly grounded with existing tools: automata-based techniques for LTL$_f$ to carry out logical reasoning, and off-the-shelf systems to solve systems of linear inequalities (and corresponding optimization problems) to handle probabilities.

In [6], beside a concrete implementation of the techniques presented in this paper, we investigate the application of probabilistic business constraints to process mining, not only considering standard problems like discovery, but also delving into online operational support and, in particular, process monitoring [4].

References

1. De Giacomo, G., De Masellis, R., Grasso, M., Maggi, F.M., Montali, M.: Monitoring Business Metaconstraints Based on LTL and LDL for Finite Traces. In: Sadiq, S., Soffer, P., Völzer, H. (eds.) BPM 2014. LNCS, vol. 8659, pp. 1–17. Springer, Cham (2014). https://doi.org/10.1007/978-3-319-10172-9_1
2. De Giacomo, G., Vardi, M.Y.: Linear temporal logic and linear dynamic logic on finite traces. In: Proceedings of the 23rd International Joint Conference on Artificial Intelligence, Beijing, China, August 3–9, IJCAI 2013, pp. 854–860, AAAI Press (2013). http://www.aaai.org/ocs/index.php/IJCAI/IJCAI13/paper/view/6997
3. Leemans, S.J.J., Syring, A.F., van der Aalst, W.M.P.: Earth movers' stochastic conformance checking. In: Hildebrandt, T., van Dongen, B.F., Röglinger, M., Mendling, J. (eds.) BPM 2019. LNBIP, vol. 360, pp. 127–143. Springer, Cham (2019). https://doi.org/10.1007/978-3-030-26643-1_8
4. Maggi, F.M., Montali, M., van der Aalst, W.M.P.: An operational decision support framework for monitoring business constraints. In: de Lara, J., Zisman, A. (eds.) FASE 2012. LNCS, vol. 7212, pp. 146–162. Springer, Heidelberg (2012). https://doi.org/10.1007/978-3-642-28872-2_11
5. Maggi, F.M., Montali, M., Peñaloza, R.: Temporal logics over finite traces with uncertainty. In: The Thirty-Fourth - AAAI Conference on Artificial Intelligence, AAAI 2020, The Thirty-Second Innovative Applications of Artificial Intelligence Conference, IAAI 2020, The Tenth - AAAI Symposium on Educational Advances in Artificial Intelligence, EAAI 2020, New York, USA, February 7–12, pp. 10218–10225 (2020). https://aaai.org/ojs/index.php/AAAI/article/view/6583
6. Maggi, F.M., Montali, M., Peñaloza, R., Alman, A.: Extending temporal business constraints with uncertainty. In: Business Process Management - 18th International Conference, BPM 2020, September 13–18. pp. 1–20, Sevilla, Spain (2020). https://doi.org/10.1007/978-3-030-58666-9
7. Montali, M., Pesic, M., van der Aalst, W.M.P., Chesani, F., Mello, P., Storari, S.: Declarative specification and verification of service choreographies. TWEB 4(1), 1–62 (2010). https://doi.org/10.1145/1658373.1658376
8. Pesic, M., Schonenberg, H., van der Aalst, W.M.P.: DECLARE: full support for loosely-structured processes. In: Proceedings of the 11th - IEEE International Enterprise Distributed Object Computing Conference (EDOC 2007), 15–19 October, pp. 287–300. Annapolis, USA (2007). https://doi.org/10.1109/EDOC.2007.14

A Method for Managing GDPR Compliance in Business Processes

Raimundas Matulevičius[1]([✉]), Jake Tom[1], Kaspar Kala[2,3], and Eduard Sing[4]

[1] Institute of Computer Science, University of Tartu, Tartu, Estonia
{rma,jaketom}@ut.ee
[2] School of Law, University of Tartu, Tartu, Estonia
kaspar.kala@ut.ee
[3] Proud Engineers OÜ, Viimsi Parish, Estonia
[4] Fujitsu Estonia AS, Tallinn, Estonia
ecbyu7@gmail.com

Abstract. Organisational compliance with the General Data Protection Regulation (GDPR) is a challenging task. In this paper, we present a GDPR model and its supporting method to manage compliance to the regulation in business processes. Based on a running example, we illustrate how the method is applied to extract an *as-is* compliance model that describes non-compliance issues and offers solutions to achieve process compliance. The GDPR model and its method are supported by a software tool. Their feasibility and validity are studied in a few business-oriented cases. The paper also discusses the model completeness with respect to the regulation.

Keywords: GDPR · Privacy management · Regulation compliance · Business process modelling

1 Introduction

With the Generic Data Protection Regulation (GDPR) [1], organisations require techniques to assess and to make compliant their state of personal data processing. Regardless of industry or size, one needs to find ways to achieve and maintain the specified privacy standards. But as there is no standard approach for achieving GDPR compliance, it is important to develop an understanding of how the privacy status can be assessed. Failing to meet compliance requirements may result in administrative fines (see [6] where more than 300 cases of the administrative fines are already reported after the GDPR introduction).

In this paper, we discuss the GDPR model [7,12] and its application to achieve the compliance in business processes. The objective is to explain *how regulation compliance could be achieved using tool-supported model-based approach*. Based on the illustrative example, we present a *method to achieve the regulation compliance*. The method supports extraction of the *as-is* compliance status, explanation and reasoning of the non-compliance issues, and change of

© Springer Nature Switzerland AG 2020
N. Herbaut and M. La Rosa (Eds.): CAiSE Forum 2020, LNBIP 386, pp. 100–112, 2020.
https://doi.org/10.1007/978-3-030-58135-0_9

the business process model in order to resolve the non-compliance issues. In addition we discuss completeness and validity of both the GDPR model and method.

The paper is structured as follows: first we present the related work (Sect. 2). In Sect. 3 we discuss the GDPR model. In Sect. 4, the method to achieve compliance is presented using the *Tollgate* scenario. Finally, Sect. 5 discusses the contribution and future research directions.

2   Related Work

Introduction of the GDPR regulation resulted in development of methods to support the regulation compliance. In [9] authors introduce the GDPR-based privacy vocabulary for data interoperability when creating privacy policies. In [8] a data labelling model for access control of privacy-critical data is defined. It uses the Fusion/UML process to design GDPR compliant system. Elsewhere, a reference model [4] for depicting the GDPR principles is defined. It helps consolidating the regulatory and business points of view using the enterprise architecture models.

In [13] a UML representation of GDPR for assessing compliance is proposed. Authors separate between the generic and contextual variations (related to the national levels) and introduce a model driven approach to support compliance activities. The study gives a strong background for the automatic analysis, however this still remains the future work. In addition the completeness of the GDPR representation is rather limited with respect to the regulation.

3   GDPR Model

The GDPR regulation introduces the major principles for the personal data processing. But it is rather broad and leaves a room for interpretation. In Fig. 1 we present the GDPR model [7,12]. *Personal data* [1] (Art. 4(1)) is represented with the class PersonalData. Data processing [1] (Art. 4(2)) is captured with the DataProcessing class, which also covers the cross-border processing [1] (Art. 4(23)) of personal data (using member_states and main_establishment attributes).

Controllers can also be *Processors*, (see, is_processor in Controller class following the Art. 28(10)), but they can't be processor and controller at the same time. The LegalGround presents that *data processing* must have a legal ground (whether consent or other). Consent is seen as a separate class that manifests one legal ground. The LegalGround, in turn, guides DataProcessing by setting the limits to the processing of personal data. Classes LegalGroundDataTransfer, LegalGroundSpecialCategory, and DataProtectionImpactAssessment represent regulation Art. 45–59, 9(2) and 35–36 respectively. The model also includes an obligation to issue the notification in case of a data breach (see, DataBreach-Notification). The ProcessingLog artefact is created to meet [1] Art. 30, which requires maintenance of records of the processing activities.

Technical measures [1] (Art. 32(1)) are represented with the TechnicalMeasures class. TechnicalMeasures has two attributes category and stereotype which, based on a taxonomy [10], could capture privacy enhancing technology means to reach privacy goals. The OrganisationalMeasures class describes how Controller should apply the organisational measures to *Data processing*. The model also describes the data processing principles and the principle of accountability (e.g., Controller *isAccountable* to PrinciplesOfProcessing) as described in [1] Art. 5.

Rights: The GDPR model also presents the *data subjects'* rights and associations (see [7,12]). The Controller is the key actor as it is responsible for enabling the data subjects' rights (i.e., Controller *enablesExercise* on Right). The regulation [1] Art. 16 defines the right of the data subject to have his/her personal data rectified when relevant. This further links to the notification obligation [1] Art. 19. Other rights, e.g., regarding *informing, objecting* and *not being subject to automated decision* – cover [1] Art. 13, 14, 21 and 22 respectively.

4 Method for Achieving Compliance

The method for achieving GDPR compliance consists of four steps, presented in Fig. 2. First, one needs to check the current level of process compliance. This includes analysis of the business process and extraction of the GDPR model instance of the current state (see, *Extract AS-IS compliance model*). Next (see, *Compare two models*), one compares the extracted model to the GDPR model. The result of the third step (see, *Define compliance issues*) is a list of the non-compliance issues. Depending on these issues, one makes a decision whether the model is compliant or not. In case of non-compliance, in the fourth step one *changes the business process model* so that the non-compliance in removed from the model. The compliance checking, then, continues with the first step taking the updated business process model as the input. Below we discuss how the method for achieving regulation compliance is applied in the *Tollgate scenario*.

Tollgate Scenario. Let's consider a *connected vehicle case*, where driver is able to enter her personal information (e.g., Bank account info) to the car, see Fig. 3. This data is then stored in the Storage of Bank account info. When the Car approaches the Tollgate, it receives a payment request from the Tollgate. The Car sends the Payment info (i.e., the driver's name and her account number). The Tollgate processes the transaction by requesting the payment from the Bank (see Request payment). The Transaction details include driver's name, bank account, tollgate ID, and amount. The Bank performs the payment transaction and informs about its success both the Tollgate (see, Inform about successful transaction and the Driver (see, Inform about transaction). Once Tollgate receives a message about the successful transaction, it allows the Car to pass (see, Pass tollgate).

Extract AS-IS Compliance Model. The input for this step is the business model, which compliance should be checked, and the GDPR model, which is used to guide the extraction of the AS-IS model. The extraction includes identification of the following GDPR model elements:

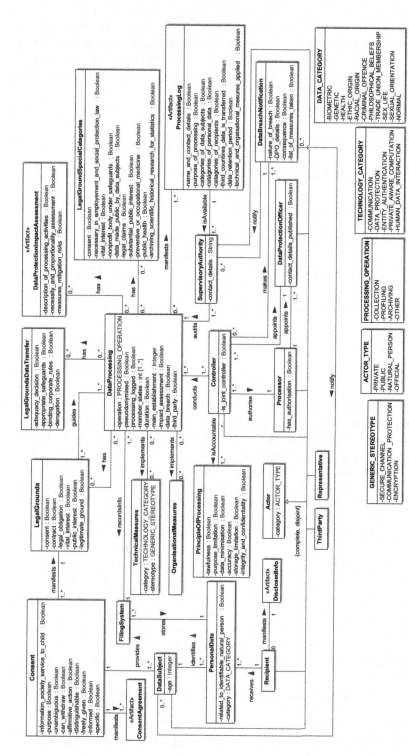

Fig. 1. GDPR model (adapted from [7,12])

Actor: The Tollgate is a *Controller*, because it "determines the purposes and means of the processing of personal data" [1]. The Tollgate is a public organisation. It does not conduct regular and systematic monitoring of data subjects (i.e., Drivers) on a large scale nor process sensitive personal data on a large scale as a core activity (see, [1] Art. 37(1)).

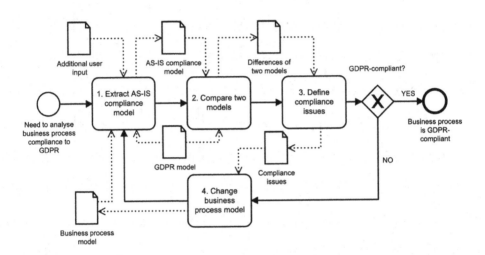

Fig. 2. Method for achieving regulation compliance, adapted from [7,11]

Personal data and *Data subject:* As illustrated in Fig. 3, the Driver is a *Data subject* because she owns the Bank account info (i.e., *Personal data*), which could be used to identify natural person (see, [1] Art. 4(1)). The Bank account info is not sensitive personal data (category is *NORMAL*).

Filling system: The filling system is the Car (information) system, where the Driver stores her Bank account info (see Fig. 3). It is, then, accessed by the Tollgate as the Payment info (see Fig. 4) is received from the car and processed.

Processing activity: The data processing activity is Request payment. This is a data collection activity (i.e., operation = *COLLECTION*). The case does not indicate whether the payment is logged (processing_logged = *FALSE*). The Payment info is transferred to other member states (i.e., Bank) thus member_state equals to 1. There is no information about a data breach (data_breach = *FALSE*).

Records of processing: The *Tollgate* process does not include any activities to record data processing. RequestPaymentLog attributes receive *FALSE* value.

Legal grounds: The *tollgate* business process (see Fig. 3 and 4) does not indicate what legal grounds ([1] Art. 6(1)) for Request payment are. The Tollgate should potentially receive the Driver's consent (see, reg. Article 6(1)(a)) for processing the Transaction details and other attributes of LegalGroundsToRequest-Payment receive value *FALSE*.

Measures: The organisational (i.e., TollgateOrgMeasures) and technical (i.e., TollgateTechMeasures) measures ([1] Art. 32) cannot be read from Fig. 3 or 4.

Disclosure: As a result of the Request payment, the Bank gets the Transaction details, which include *driver name*, his *bank account, tollgate ID* (which could be seen as a sensitive information as it reveals driver's location) and payed *amount*.

Principle of processing: As there is no conflicting information, it is presumed that the Tollgate (as the *Controller*) follows the data processing principles (see, [1] Art. 5(1)).

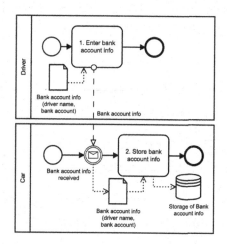

Fig. 3. Tollgate scenario: data input

Data subject rights: Let's assume that Driver wishes to rectify his Bank account info (e.g., process in Fig. 3) in the Car (see, [1] Art. 16). Figure 5 illustrates this situation, also by covering the [1] Art. 12(3)–12(6) (i.e., identity_confirmed, action_taken_within_30_days and free_of_charge both get assigned *TRUE* value).

Compare two Models and Define Compliance Issues. Table 1 presents an extract of comparison of two – the GDPR and the AS-IS – models. The instance of ProcessingLog is RequestPaymentLog. Following the [1] Art. 30(1), "each controller <...> shall maintain a record of processing activity" [1]. This is not the case in the *Tollgate* example, where logging activity is not present. Thus, the non-compliance (NC#1) issue is identified suggesting that the activity of logging needs to be introduced. The log should include the controller's name (Tollgate), purpose of processing (payment for passing the tollgate), data subject category (Driver name), personal data category (bank account info: *NORMAL*), recipient category (Bank), and the applied technical and organisational measures.

Following Art. 6(1), the processing needs to be lawful (see, correspondence between the LegalGrounds and LegalGroundsToRequestPayment) "only if and to the extent that at least one" [1] of the LegalGroundsToRequestPayment attributes receives value *TRUE*. If not, then the Consent (i.e., DriverConsent) should be given by the Data subject (i.e., Driver) "to the processing of his or her personal data for one or more specific purposes" [1]. The non-compliance issue (NC#2) is defined to indicate that the *Tollgate* case does not illustrate how the consent is given (or is there any other indications of the RequestPayment lawfulness).

Following the Art. 32(1), "the controller <...> shall implement appropriate technical and organisational measures to ensure a level of security" [1]. The TollgateOrgMeasures corresponds to OrganisationalMeasures in the GDPR model and TollgateTechMeasures – to TechnicalMeasures. However, neither TollgateOrgMeasures nor OrganisationalMeasures are defined (or visualised) in the *Tollgate* case, thus this situation results in another non-compliance issue (NC#3).

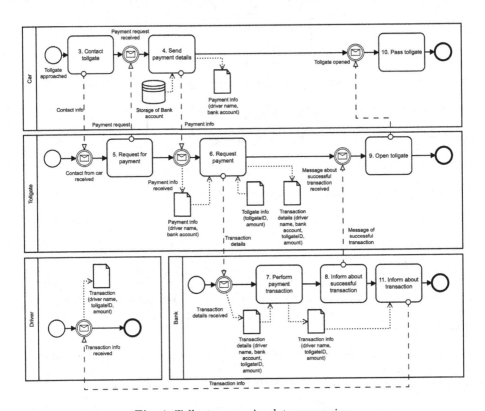

Fig. 4. Tollgate scenario: data processing

Change Business Process Model. Figure 6 and 7 illustrate how identified non-compliance issues are addressed in the *Tollgate* example.

NC#1: To address the first non-compliance issue, the Tollgate should contain a storage of the Logs of Request payment (see, Fig. 7). After performance of the Request payment activity, the Tollgate logs the request transaction details (see, activity C2). Besides the Transaction details, the log entry should also include the *purpose of processing, recipient* (i.e., Bank), *technical* (e.g., *cryptographic means*, see below) and organisational measures.

NC#2: The second non-compliance is addressed by introducing how *Driver's consent* is handled to the Tollgate. In Fig. 6, while entering the Bank account details, the driver should also Provide the consent to process Bank account details (see activity *C1.2*). The consent is then placed in the storage contained in the Car (information system). When processing the Payment info (see, Fig. 7), the Tollgate checks the driver's consent validity (see, activity *C1.4*). If it is not valid, the Tollgate informs driver about the invalid consent (see, activity C1.5), otherwise it proceeds with the data processing activity (see, Request payment).

NC#3: In the *tollgate* example we discuss one set of technical measures. In Fig. 6, activity *C3.1* illustrates that the Bank account info should be encrypted. The encrypted data are stored in the Car (information system). Then, in Fig. 7, the Tollgate receives it from the Car (see, Payment info) and submits it to the Bank (see, Transaction details). The Bank uses the Private key to decrypt the Bank account info in order to perform the payment transaction.

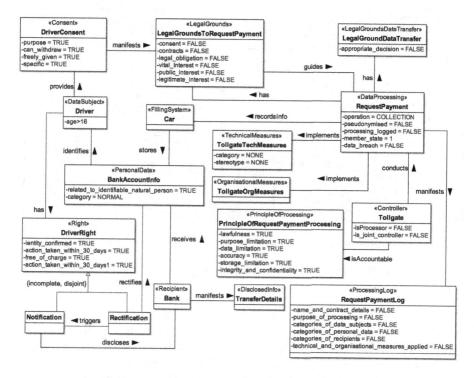

Fig. 5. Tollgate scenario: AS-IS compliance model

5   Discussion and Concluding Remarks

Tool Support. To support the GDPR compliance method (see Sect. 4), a prototype tool (see, https://github.com/motekaj/gdpr-analyzer) [11] is implemented.

Table 1. Table captions should be placed above the tables.

Reg. article	GDPR model	AS-IS compliance model	Non-compliance issue
30(1)	ProcessingLog	RequestPaymentLog	NC#1
6(1)	LegalGrounds	LegalGroundsToRequestPayment	NC#2
6(1)	Consent	DriverConsent	NC#2
32(1)	OrganisationMeasures	TollgateOrgMeasure	NC#3
32(1)	TechnicalMeasures	TollgateTechMeasure	NC#3

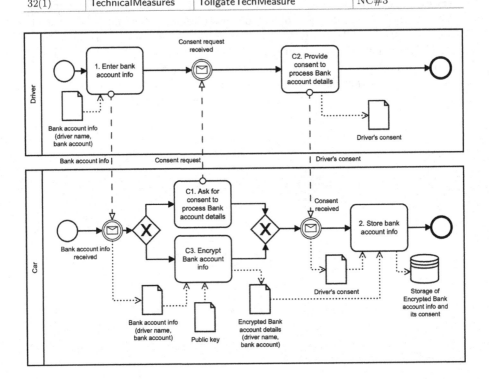

Fig. 6. Tollgate scenario: non-compliance resolution for data input

The main functions of the prototype support the method for achieving regulation compliance (see, Fig. 2) and include (step 1) extraction of the AS-IS compliance model, (step 2) comparison of the two models, and (step 3) definition of compliance issues. The tool helps to detect the non-compliance issues as *flags* attached to the relevant model elements and lists the recommended guidelines to address them in the business process model. The updated model should be the input to the next iteration of the compliance checking (i.e., step 1 of the method).

Limitation. The GDPR model does not consider how it may be adapted in a national context. The GDPR leaves a room for Member States to deviate on some aspects (including the legal grounds of processing that may arise from the

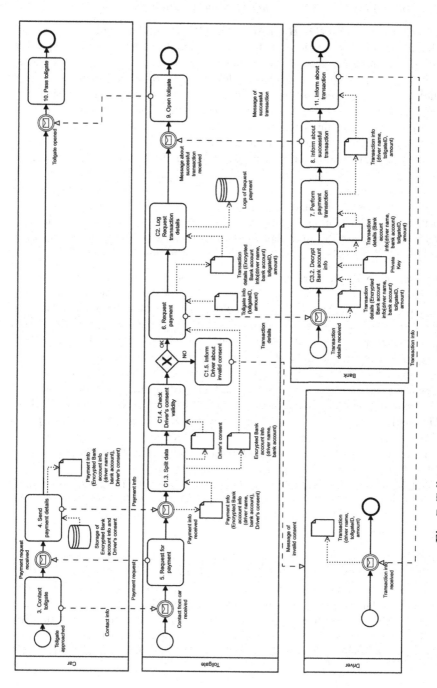

Fig. 7. Tollgate scenario: non-compliance resolution for data processing

national laws). The model would have to be adjusted when there are aspects that controller must take into account to achieve compliance.

Completeness of the GDPR Model. The GDPR regulation includes 99 articles (including 191 (sub)articles in total), but not all articles consider specific legal requirements for organisations. Some articles contain generic effort clauses that are not fit for modelling. The model given in Fig. 1 addresses only the specific[1] legal requirements obliging controllers and processors. In addition the GDPR model includes several special cases concerning the applicability criteria which are presented using the BPMN notations in [7]. The additional applicability criteria are (*i*) conducting a data protection impact assessment or prior consultation with the supervisory authority [1] Art. 35 and 36; (*ii*) processing of special categories of data on a legal basis [1] Art. 9(2); (*iii*) transferring personal data to a third country [1] Art. 45(1), 46(1), 46(2), 46(3), 47(1) and 49(1); (*iv*) making a data breach notification in case of a data breach [1] Art. 33 and 34.

In total the GDPR model (see details in [7]) concerns 40 articles (including 75 (sub)articles) resulting in rather high completeness (in comparison to other works [4,9,13]) while checking the compliance of the business processes.

Administrative Fines. Organisations want to be compliant in order to avoid administrative fines. Non-compliance of the data processing principles is a main infringement under [1] Art. 83(5)(a). The GDPR model includes analysis of *legal ground*, *legal ground special categories* and *legal ground data transfer*, which guides the *data processing*. The *legal ground special category* and *legal ground data transfer* define the legality of processing special data categories [1] Art. 9(2) and the legality of data transfers to third countries. The model includes all the *data subject rights* which cover [1] Art. 12(3)–12(6) and helps avoiding fines.

The *data processing* and *accountability* principles [1] Art. 5 are included, too. The obligation to conduct a *data protection impact assessment* and *prior consultation* enable the organisation to decide whether these needs to be conducted and if so, what are the content requirements. The *data processing* also includes three attributes for *impact assessment*, [1] Art. 33–35, *data breach* [1] Art. 45(1), 46(1), 46(3), 47(1) and *third country* [1] Art. 49(1). Besides the *technical measures*, the GDPR model also considers the *organisational measures* [1] Art. 32(1), 25(1) and 25(2). Addressing these compliance issues minimises the risk of incurring administrative fines.

Validity. In addition to the *tollgate* scenario, the GDPR model, its supporting method and tool have been applied in a few other cases. In [5], the GDPR model is used to support modelling of the goal-actor-rule perspective. The study shows how modelling language could be extended to capture infringement and to solve it using embodiment, finding irregularities, compliance checking and irregularity resolution activities. In [2] the GDPR model is applied in an airline contact centre processes. The results of both cases [5] and [2] were introduced to the

---

[1] The ones, which can be represented using UML activity, association or class notations.

domain experts who found the application of the GDPR model intuitive and helpful to achieve business process compliance.

In [11] the manual application of the method to achieve regulation compliance is compared to the tool-supported analysis. The results indicate a high correspondence between the number of found non-compliance issues. In addition the tool-supported application is able to highlight non-compliance issues (e.g., application of the technical measures), which were omitted from the manual analysis.

Future Work. Both, the GDPR model and method for achieving compliance needs further refinement. Future research is also needed for tool support regarding the *change of the business process model* (see Step 4, Fig. 2). Potentially, *process design patterns* [3] could be useful, but one needs to define the link between the identified non-compliance issues and the available patterns.

Acknowledgement. This paper is supported in part by European Union's Horizon 2020 research and innovation programme under grant agreement No 830892, project SPARTA. We would like also to thank Manon Knockaert (*University of Namur*) for the constructive comments while preparing this paper.

References

1. EU General Data Protection Regulation. https://eur-lex.europa.eu/legal-content/EN/TXT/?uri=uriserv:OJ.L.2016.119.01.0001.01.ENG
2. Abbasi, A.: GDPR implementation in an airline contact center. Master's thesis, University of Tartu (2018)
3. Agostinelli, S., Maggi, F.M., Marrella, A., Sapio, F.: Achieving GDPR compliance of BPMN process models. In: Cappiello, C., Ruiz, M. (eds.) CAiSE 2019. LNBIP, vol. 350, pp. 10–22. Springer, Cham (2019). https://doi.org/10.1007/978-3-030-21297-1_2
4. Blanco-Lainé, G., Sottet, J.-S., Dupuy-Chessa, S.: Using an enterprise architecture model for GDPR compliance principles. In: Gordijn, J., Guédria, W., Proper, H.A. (eds.) PoEM 2019. LNBIP, vol. 369, pp. 199–214. Springer, Cham (2019). https://doi.org/10.1007/978-3-030-35151-9_13
5. Çelebi, I.: Privacy enhanced secure Tropos: a privacy modeling language for GDPR compliance. Master's thesis, University of Tartu (2018)
6. C'M'S': GDPR Enforcement Tracker. https://enforcementtracker.com/
7. Kala, K.: Refinement of the general data protection regulation (GDPR) model: administrative fines perspective. Master's thesis, University of Tartu (2019)
8. Kammüller, F., Ogunyanwo, O.O., Probst, C.W.: Designing data protection for GDPR compliance into IoT healthcare systems. arXiv:1901.02426 (2019, in submitted)
9. Pandit, H.J., et al.: Creating a vocabulary for data privacy. In: Panetto, H., Debruyne, C., Hepp, M., Lewis, D., Ardagna, C.A., Meersman, R. (eds.) OTM 2019. LNCS, vol. 11877, pp. 714–730. Springer, Cham (2019). https://doi.org/10.1007/978-3-030-33246-4_44
10. Pullonen, P., Tom, J., Matulevičius, R., Toots, A.: Privacy-enhanced BPMN: enabling data privacy analysis in business processes models. Softw. Syst. Model. **18**(6), 3235–3264 (2019)

11. Sing, E.: Meta-model driven method for establishing business process compliance to GDPR. Master's thesis, University of Tartu (2018)
12. Tom, J., Sing, E., Matulevičius, R.: Conceptual representation of the GDPR: model and application directions. In: Zdravkovic, J., Grabis, J., Nurcan, S., Stirna, J. (eds.) BIR 2018. LNBIP, vol. 330, pp. 18–28. Springer, Cham (2018). https://doi.org/10.1007/978-3-319-99951-7_2
13. Torre, D., Soltana, G., Sabetzadeh, M., Briand, L.C., Auffinger, Y., Goes, P.: Using models to enable compliance checking against the GDPR: an experience report. In: Proceedings of the 22nd International Conference on Model Driven Engineering Languages and Systems (MODELS 19) (2019)

Why It Is Time for Yet Another Schema Evolution Benchmark
Visionary Paper

Mark Lukas Möller[1]([⊠]), Stefanie Scherzinger[2], Meike Klettke[1],
and Uta Störl[3]

[1] University of Rostock, Rostock, Germany
{mark.moeller2,meike.klettke}@uni-rostock.de
[2] University of Passau, Passau, Germany
stefanie.scherzinger@uni-passau.de
[3] Darmstadt University of Applied Sciences, Darmstadt, Germany
uta.stoerl@h-da.de

Abstract. Database schema evolution is one of the grand challenges in
data management research and practice. In this paper, we survey available schema evolution benchmarks. We argue that existing benchmarks
do not reflect the more recent demands on database applications, such
as online data migration for high availability applications, agile release
strategies, and schema changes that affect more than one data model.
We conclude that a new generation of schema evolution benchmarks is
called for, which reflect these new demands, especially in the context of
schema evolution in NoSQL data stores.

Keywords: Evolution benchmarks · Schema transformation · NoSQL

1 Introduction

Schema evolution is a timeless topic in database research, with publications
dating back over 40 years [5,18]; nevertheless, the topic has not lost its relevance among researchers (c.f. [10]) and practitioners (c.f. [2]). Managing schema
evolution becomes even more urgent with the movement to be agile in application development: Being lean, committing to decisions as late as possible—
also concerning the schema—is in stark contrast to the "schema first" doctrine
that we have been teaching in database textbooks and classrooms for decades.
Schema evolution not only comprises the changes to the schema itself, captured
by schema evolution operations (SMOs), but also requires a strategy for migrating data accordingly. For instance, data can be migrated eagerly, lazily, or in
a hybrid combination of both. A schema evolution benchmark can help with
finding a suitable data migration strategy.

In this paper, we survey the current landscape of schema evolution benchmarks. We point out specific weaknesses when applying them to database applications with modern software stacks. Today, many database applications often

N. Herbaut and M. La Rosa (Eds.): CAiSE Forum 2020, LNBIP 386, pp. 113–125, 2020.
https://doi.org/10.1007/978-3-030-58135-0_10

need to be available 24/7 and do not allow for convenient time windows where large-scale data migrations can occur (such as a weekend or a bank holiday). For agile development teams, the benchmarks must mimic frequent and incremental schema changes. Further, modern applications often employ novel (possibly even several) data models, as they may be backed by NoSQL data stores, multi-model data stores, or even poly-stores. When the data store is schema-free, we may even have to work with versioned data [8,9] within the same database (rather than a combination of databases with different schemas). Moreover, many applications store *Big Data*, and schema evolution benchmarks should reflect this.

We show that available benchmarks, many designed for more traditional database applications, are found wanting when scrutinized under these new requirements. This leads us to make our case towards designing yet another schema evolution benchmark for researchers working on schema evolution.

CONTRIBUTIONS. We analyze existing schema evolution benchmarks and big data analytics benchmarks to find out their similarities as well as the best practices for benchmarks. We characterize these benchmarks systematically (a) whether the scenario is synthetic or based on real-world data; (b) the availability and repeatability of the benchmark data; (c) the data model and queries; and (d) the year of publication of the benchmark (an indicator of its maturity), as well as the citations of the publications as a proxy metric for their adoption.

2 Schema Evolution and Data Migration Strategies

Software products undergo code changes. This includes frequent evolutions of data structures in the source core which in turn implies the necessity to eventually adapt the schema of the application-backing database and its legacy data to such data model changes [13]. Typically, schema evolution encompasses two steps. Firstly, the schema of the data is adapted and a new schema version is introduced. Secondly, the existing data in the old schema version is transformed to match the new schema. So-called *schema modification operations (SMOs)* describe schema changes and their effects (c.f. [20]).

Numerous empirical studies exist on how schemas evolve in real projects. One subject of study is MediaWiki, the software behind Wikipedia, which was intensively studied in the *Pantha Rei* benchmark (c.f. [4]). The authors investigated the differences between schema changes and distinguished them into *macro* changes referring to the type of the operation, e.g. schema changes or index changes, and *micro changes* referring to actual schema changes on the extracted SMOs. The SMOs which occurred most frequently across all schema versions are visualized in Fig. 1.

Apparently, the most frequent operations are column based operations, while table based operations occur rarely, with the exception of the create table SMO. Another empirical study in [16] addresses the impact of SMOs. Changes in ten open source database applications were analyzed and classified into multiple categories. It was shown that the most common operations were *transformations*

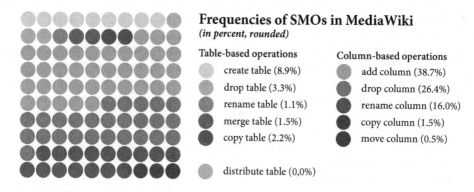

Frequencies of SMOs in MediaWiki
(in percent, rounded)

Table-based operations

- create table (8.9%)
- drop table (3.3%)
- rename table (1.1%)
- merge table (1.5%)
- copy table (2.2%)

Column-based operations

- add column (38.7%)
- drop column (26.4%)
- rename column (16.0%)
- copy column (1.5%)
- move column (0.5%)

- distribute table (0,0%)

Fig. 1. SMOs and their frequency across MediaWiki schema versions, (c.f. [4])

(e.g. adding a column) and *structural refactoring operations* (e.g. dropping a table). Only one application constituted an exception where the most changes consisted of adding default values [16]. We can conclude that table-related or column-related operations are the most frequent operations and thus, have to play a major role in schema evolution benchmarks.

There are different strategies for the data migration which are executing the SMO for the datasets. In general, we can distinguish between *eager data migration, lazy migration* [20], and *hybrid migration* [11,13] approaches. In *eager migration* all datasets are instantaneously migrated into the latest schema version whenever a SMO is executed. This migration strategy occasions high costs for the update operations because all datasets are immediately migrated, including those currently not in use. In *lazy migration* the schema modification is executed only if the dataset is requested by the application. Therefore, lazy data migration migrates *on-demand*, updating only so-called 'hot' data. The general observation can be made that a lazy data migration strategy reduces the update costs but increases the prospective latency when datasets are requested. Some applications, however, apply a *no migration* approach where data migration is not materialized. Here, all datasets are kept in their original version even if requested, and queries have to be rewritten against the latest schema version in order to match. A query rewriting algorithm for NoSQL databases has been proposed in [15]. For other settings, a *hybrid migration* has been suggested as a compromise between eager and lazy migration [11]. Here, datasets are migrated that are predicted to be accessed in the near future.

These data migration strategies vary significantly in their performance, operation costs, and their latency times. In [11], different metrics for established as well as for newly defined data migration strategies for NoSQL databases have been measured and visualized. Now, a schema evolution benchmark has to be applied in order to evaluate the performance and compare the efficiency of the different data migration strategies.

3   Benchmark Characteristics

In the scope of this article, we compare five systems which are either benchmarks or related systems. We compare them in detail regarding their *data model*, their *queries or workload*, their *data generator* and *data availability* (if the set of original data used for the benchmark is still available) and their *metrics*. A side-to-side comparison is made in Table 1 while the details are described in the next sections. The five systems we regard are the following:

Pantha Rei [4]. The first schema evolution benchmark is *Pantha Rei* which benchmarks MediaWiki. It is surveyed since the authors derive SMOs for an existing system and benchmark the query correctness (c.f. Sect. 4.1).

Twente [25]. The benchmark from *University of Twente* extends the TPC-C benchmark by introducing complex schema transformations.

STBenchmark [1] is a benchmark for mapping systems. These systems allow to describe relationships between multiple schemas, e.g. for information integration (c.f. [1]). We include it in our survey since the key ideas of mapping systems share many commonalities with schema evolution systems.

BigBench (TPCx-BB) [6]. The *BigBench (TPCx-BB)* is not a schema evolution benchmark, however, it encompasses big data aspects, a variety of data ranging from structured to unstructured data, an extensive description of the queries, and a detailed documentation.

Unibench [27] does not deal with schema evolution but gives valuable insights in how to deal with several data models.

In the next sections, we provide more detailed insights into the characteristics of the five above mentioned benchmarks with regards to the mentioned characteristics, starting with the data model.

3.1   Data Model

Since the data model changes over time due to evolution, the data model only holds for a certain point in time.

Based on an empirical study on schema changes in MediaWiki, the database application behind Wikipedia, the benchmark *Pantha Rei* was crafted. It relies on the relational MediaWiki schema. The schema currently consists of 48 tables divided into 13 categories, e.g., 7 tables for storing user data and 4 tables to store multimedia information. While MediaWiki supports multiple database backends, MySQL is used as the basis for Pantha Rei [4].

The *Twente* benchmark [25] is an extension of the TPC-C benchmark from 2010, containing basic and complex schema transformations. TPC-C represents an OLTP benchmark and models an order management system of a company with multiple warehouses in different districts. While the TPC-C benchmark is augmented with newly introduced schema transformation operations, the schema is not adapted and contains 9 tables. For the underlying DBMS, MySQL and PostgresQL was used. The database was generated using HammerDB (c.f. [25]).

The *STBenchmark* is an approach for benchmarking mapping systems. Often, it is required to model relationships between different schemas. Because

Table 1. Classification of schema evolution systems and benchmarks.

	Pantha Rei	Twente	STBenchmark	BigBench	Unibench
Basic Information					
Publishing year	2008	2015	2008	2013	2018
Citations of Reference	115 of [4]	2 of [25]	154 of [1]	325 of [6]	8 of [27]
Type of data model					
Single Model	MediaWiki	TPC-C	BioWarehouse (among others)	–	–
Multi Model	–	–	–	TPCx-BB	Social Warehouse
Type of data					
Structured	✓	✓	–	✓	✓
Semi-structured	–	–	✓	✓	✓
Unstructured	–	–	–	✓	✓
Data Availability					
Original data	(✓)*	–	–	–	–
Data generator	–	✓	✓	✓	✓
Workload					
OLTP Queries	✓	✓	–	–	✓
OLAP Queries	–	–	–	✓	✓
SMO Operations	✓	✓	–	–	–
Mapping Scenarios	–	–	✓	–	–
Metrics					
Performance	–	✓	✓	✓	✓
Robustness/Adaptivity	✓	–	–	–	–

Legend: ✓: Yes, –: No, ^{a}: On the project website, the authors refer to a MediaWiki dump page. Unfortunately, some links, e.g., to the Wikipedia on-line profiler, are no longer valid. Citation count according to Google Scholar, checked on 11/12/2019.

there are similarities between mapping and evolution (the same SMOs are applied in both cases) the benchmark is included here. For the scenarios, the benchmark adopts ideas of the TPC-H and the XMark benchmark. It consists of a set of mappings which are likely for real world mapping applications in the industry. The scenarios consists of a data model, a database instance and a set of queries based on real world applications like DBLP oder BioWarehouse.

The *TPC Express BigBench (TPCx-BB)* benchmark was designed for Big Data Analytical Systems (BDAS) and covers essential aspects of Big Data use cases. The data model represents a web sales application and contains a relational part with a multiple-snowflake schema for the key information such as customers, items and sales, a semi-structured part for the web-logs and an unstructured part for product reviews. Most of the data is stored as semi-structured or unstructured data, only 20% of the data is stored in the relational part [23] (c.f. [6]).

Unibench models a social warehouse application and simultaneously consists of a document store, a key-value store, an XML store, a relational database, and a graph store.

In [24], the authors surveyed benchmarks and distinguished between *textbook-* and *real-world-benchmarks*. They observed a gap between benchmarks proposed in textbooks and online tutorials compared to real world benchmarks which is important to keep in mind when designing a benchmark.

Observations. Unsurprisingly, the intention of all data benchmarks is to model real-world applications. While some benchmarks like TPCx-BB model systems which are realistic to occur in real-world scenarios (c.f. [17]), other benchmarks such as the MediaWiki benchmark or the STBenchmark are derived from real-world systems.

3.2 Queries and Workload

The workload can be either defined by a set of SMOs or by a set of reference queries for measuring the query success or failure rates and to determine the amount of data that is affected by an evolution operation.

The *Pantha Rei* benchmark generates multiple sets of queries. One set contains the 500 most common queries derived from the Wikipedia on-line profiler[1]. Nearly 2,500 queries are *lab-gen* queries, derived from the interaction of the frontend and the backend. Legacy *synthetic probe queries* are used to access single columns to highlight the portion of data that was affected by an evolution operation. As a metric, the success rate of queries is measured (c.f. [4]).

The *Twente* benchmark consists of 30 schema transformation operations, whereby 21 queries are considered as basic transformations, such as creating a relation, rename a column or change its data type, creating indices or constraints, and nine complex queries such as splitting or joining relations (c.f. [25]).

The workload of the *STBenchmark* consists of mapping scenarios generated by the *SGen* workload generator. The generator is parameterizable and allows to adapt parameters such as nesting depth and join size. Generally, the workload consists of tasks that are frequent in applications, such as copying records, partitioning, nesting and unnesting and object fusion (c.f. [1]).

Analogously to the data model of *BigBench*, the queries for this benchmarks are divided into queries for structured data, queries for semi-structured data, and queries for unstructured data. Despite the fact that only 20% of the data is stored in the structured part, 18 of 30 queries are executed on structured data, while 7 queries access semi-structured and 5 queries access unstructured data. The queries are relevant business cases according to McKinsey's. Even if this benchmark does not contain schema evolution, it represents an interesting approach for designing a benchmark workload (c.f. [6,23]).

Unibench provides a set of ten analytical multi-model queries.

Observations. While some approaches use complex queries or analytical queries to measure the performance of the respective systems, other approaches are generating queries to check the portion of affected data by data migration operations, triggered by SMOs and by how many queries are still working in the latest schema version. Depending on the metric, both variants are important concepts. All approaches have in common that they are using queries or statements that are typical in their specific application domain.

---

[1] Was originally http://noc.wikimedia.org/cgi-bin/report.py?db=enwiki&sort=real& limit=50000, not available anymore [11/20/2019].

3.3   Data Generator and Data Availability

The *Pantha Rei* benchmark uses the MediaWiki schema and the Wikipedia data. On the project website[2], the authors refer to a Wikipedia data dump page where datasets can be downloaded. Depending on the language, the size of the dataset is between less than 10 MB and more than 700 GB.

The *Twente* benchmark uses the TPC-C data generator and generates a data warehouse instance per DBMS according to the TPC-C specification (c.f. [25]).

STBenchmark uses IGen, a source instance generator built on top of ToX-Gene, a tool for generating XML content. As input IGen takes a parametrized, XML-like templates that describes how the content will be generated [1].

According to the TPCx-BB specification, *BigBench/TPCx-BB* comes with the *Parallel Data Generator Framework* to generate the test dataset [23].

The *Unibench* benchmark comes with the *Unigen* data generator that generates data to the hard disk. This data can be imported using the ETL-tools of the according databases.

Unfortunately, apart from the MediaWiki benchmark, we were not able to find any of the original data used for the benchmarking. Since the generators of the benchmarks create a large amount of data, it is unlikely that all parts of data has been archived.

Observations. Most benchmarks generate test data. Only the research group of MediaWiki provided a reference to a real data set. In order to combine both flexibility and reproducibility of benchmark results, we propose to provide a *parameterizable, yet deterministic data generator* that lets the user modify the way how data is generated, but generates for the same parameter setting the exact same data set for multiple generation runs.

3.4   Benchmark Metrics

Despite the fact that benchmarks provide a standardized approach for measuring performance or efficiency, the metrics of the certain benchmarks differ depending on the objectives of the benchmarks.

The *MediaWiki* benchmark executes a set of queries against the database in each schema version. It is measured for each query if it is executed successfully or not. Hence, the metrics for this benchmark is the *query success rate*. While the approach does not measure performance, it is crucial to measure the impact of a SMO with respect to the effort, i.e., how many queries are required to be changed in order to be able to work with the latest schema version (c.f. [4]).

Regarding the metrics, the *Twente* benchmark and *STBenchmark* are similar. Both use the computation time or transactions per minute as a metric and refer to it as performance (c.f. [1, 25]).

---

2 http://yellowstone.cs.ucla.edu/schema-evolution/index.php/
Benchmark_Downloadables [11/29/2019].

The metrics of the *BigBench* benchmark are executed BigBench Queries per hour (BBQpH@SF). If a scale factor is used to increase the amount of data, then *SF* represents this scale factor (c.f. [23]).

Unibench simply measures the query execution time per query.

Observations. Benchmarks do not always measure performance. Executing queries without adapting them to the new schema can help to find out which portion of data is influenced by data migration operations caused by SMOs. A query success rate can help to figure out which data migration strategy can be used and to estimate *migration debts* in case of lazy migration.

In this section, we compiled the benchmark characteristics for different systems and tried to extract their similarities and best practices. We use the results for a general concept of an own schema evolution benchmark.

4   Towards a New Schema Evolution Benchmark

Although schema evolution benchmarks differ from traditional benchmarks both types of benchmarks are not completely different with respect to their basic conceptional model. In [7], Jim Gray stated that the four main criteria are *Relevance*, *Portability*, *Scalability*, and *Simplicity*, which good benchmarks need to meet and which are applicable for schema evolution benchmarks as well.

Relevance means that a benchmark needs to cover typical operations in the application domain. Implicitly, this means that beside the queries the data model has to represent a typical application as well (c.f. [7]). *Portability* means that it must be easy to implement the benchmark for different systems and different architectures. Providing portability is necessary to make systems comprehensible regarding the benchmark metrics (c.f. [7]). *Scalability* originally describes the support on small and large computer systems, as well as on parallel computer systems (c.f. [7]). Nowadays, this demand can be adapted to big data technology, so as to support concepts such as sharded clusters in comparison to a stand-alone database. *Simplicity* describes the necessity that the benchmark has to be easy to understand as well as easy to be set up (c.f. [7]).

4.1   Requirements for a Schema Evolution Benchmark

In this section, we derive requirements for a schema evolution benchmark based on the discussed characteristics of the benchmarks in Sect. 3.

DATA MODEL. To provide extensive use cases, the schema evolution benchmark is required to consider *data variety*. Therefore, the data model consists of relational data as well as of semi- and unstructured data. Non-relational data can be parametrized regarding the nested data and optional properties.

DATA GENERATION. Benchmarking evolution primarily involves the schema. Nevertheless, generated data is important as well to benchmark the correctness and the impact of SMOs. As learned from the Pantha Rei benchmark, query robustness is an important metric and depending on the implementation of the SMOs, data might be transformed differently into the new schema version. Therefore, it is not possible to omit data generation to prove the correctness of complex queries such as aggregations after a schema modification.

QUERIES. For the query generation process, it is required to distinguish between *QL-Statements* and *SMOs* statements. The set of SMO statements consists of typical operations as mentioned in Sect. 3, modifies the schema to the latest version, and migrates data to the latest schema version. The set of QL-statements is defined on the initial schema of the benchmark and consists of read-only operations. It is used to measure the affected portion of data by an SMO. The level of adaptivity or correctness can be determined if the used schema evolution system supports query rewriting. In this case, it is possible to measure how well automatically rewritten queries fit to the new schema.

METRICS. For a schema evolution benchmark, two main metrics have been briefly addressed in the query generation section. The first metric is *performance*. If data is migrated eagerly, performance refers to the efficient immediate transformation of data from the old into the new schema. If data is migrated lazily, performance measures the on-demand transformation time of selected data, including internal optimizations, e.g., by conflating multiple applied evolution operations. The second metric is *query correctness* or *adaptability* for query rewriting. If a query against the latest schema is rewritten due to SMOs that were yet not executed on the logical level for certain entities, it is expected that the query result is the same as for an eager data migration. This metric allows to benchmark the effectivity of the query rewriting and to validate it.

Compared to Table 1, our approach can be classified as follows: We propose a benchmark covering *structured, semi-structured* as well as *unstructured* data. The benchmark comes with a *parameterizable data generator* that generates data in a deterministic way in order to provide generator-based access to the original data. The benchmark shall measure both *performance*, i.e. execution time for different kinds of SMOs, as well as *robustness*, i.e. which part of data was modified and how well rewritten queries work, if applicable.

4.2   Benchmark Core Components

Compiling the results of the previous sections and inspired by [9], we propose a 3-stage benchmark model in Fig. 2 that consists of a *benchmark preflight stage* to set up the benchmark, a *benchmark execution stage* where the actual benchmark is executed, and a *benchmark post-execution stage* with result reporting and analysis. Next, we will describe all stages and tasks in detail.

PREFLIGHT STAGE. The benchmark preflight stage requires user interaction and is for parameterizing the benchmark e.g., regarding the distribution of structured and unstructured data, the maximum nesting depth and the distribution of single- and multi-type SMOs. Because not all systems support concepts such

Benchmark Preflight	Benchmark Execution	Benchmark Post-Execution
Choice of Data Model	Schema Generation	Result Checking
Choice of SMO Queries	Data Generation	Result Reporting
Choice of Metrics	SMO Query Execution	Result In-Depth Analysis
Setup of Scale Factors	Profiling	...
Data Generator Parametrization	...	
Database Adapter Selection		
...		

Fig. 2. Core components of the benchmark

as query rewriting, the user has to choose the set of metrics. For the data generator the scale factor for the amount of generated data and characteristics like cardinalities have to be parameterized. Finally, the connection to the system to be benchmarked has to be set up. Other metrics for the preflight stage are possible, such as creating debug data (e.g. execution plans).

EXECUTION STAGE. The benchmark execution stage is a stage without user interaction. Here, the schema and data is generated with respect to the settings of the previous stage. Afterwards, the SMOs are executed. During the whole process a profiling task monitors the steps regarding time, memory, and CPU consumption. Other parameters like the execution environment (on-premise vs. cloud-based) can be important as well as shown in [11].

POST-EXECUTION STAGE. The post-execution stage involves result checking and reporting. In the result report, values about CPU, memory, and time consumption are shown per SMO/query. If adaptivity was chosen as a metric in the preflight stage, it is reported which part of data was influenced by the SMOs and which part of data the query rewriting routine actually covered. Created debug data can be analyzed in-depth and logs ensure provenance aspects because they allow to track how certain results were generated.

In this section we introduced the core components of a benchmark and its high-level requirements, rather than in-depth technicalities. The next step in our future research is to craft a specific schema evolution scenario.

5   Related Work

Because benchmarks are highly domain-specific, there is no one-benchmark-fits-all solution and a variety of benchmarks has been developed in the past. One of the most valuable resources is "The Benchmark Handbook For Database And Transaction Processing Systems" by Jim Gray [7]. It explains key criteria for benchmarks and analyzes several benchmarks in detail. The TPC benchmarks from the *Transaction Processing Council* are well-known and standards or de-facto standards for benchmarking systems. There is a variety of benchmarks, ranging from OLTP benchmarks (*TPC-C*, *TPC-E*) and data integration benchmarks (*TPC-DI*) to Big Data benchmarks, such as *TPCx-BB* or *TPCx-HS* [22]. The TPC benchmarks have been designed without schema evolution support, however. *PolyBench* claims to be *the first benchmark for polystores* and benchmarks heterogeneous analytics systems. Polystores are unions of multiple specialized systems, i.e., structured and unstructured systems are combined to model a banking business model [12]. Other benchmarks are for example the *Bucky* and the *007* benchmark for object-oriented databases, and *YCSB* for NoSQL systems (c.f. [3]). Non of these has been developed for schema evolution but they can be inspiring concerning their designs and concepts.

Schema evolution has been present as a topic for decades. Roddick surveyed schema version issues and evolving database systems in 1995 already [18]. Similar to the examined approaches in Sect. 2, the authors of [14] investigated the effects of schema evolution on applications. Analogously to the empirical evaluations in [4] and [16], the main focus relies on table and attribute changes. Similar studies can be found in [26] and [21]. In [19], the schema evolution approach *KVolve* is introduced which was evaluated using the default Redis performance benchmark as a micro-benchmark, and *redisfs* and *Amico* as macro benchmark [19]. Another approach for database evolution is offered through *InVerDa* using a database evolution language supporting query rewriting (c.f. [10]).

6   Conclusion and Outlook

Despite schema evolution being so important, only few dedicated benchmarks are available. Even consortiums such as the TPC have not provided an evolution benchmark, although many research groups emphasized its importance. Moreover, existing benchmarks have turned out to be incomplete, largely due to the fact that benchmarks like Pantha Rei happen to be byproducts of publications not designed to support various of experiments. Consequently, we call for building a new benchmark that can be used for testing a much larger range of schema evolution tasks.

We summarized the features of several well-known database benchmarks, with a focus on schema evolution. We identified best practices, as well as limitations, and proposed requirements for a standardized schema evolution benchmark. While this article gives an overview of the concepts, we dedicate ourselves to propose a technically detailed benchmark acknowledging our results.

References

1. Alexe, B., Tan, W.C., Velegrakis, Y.: STBenchmark: towards a benchmark for mapping systems. PVLDB 1(1), 230–244 (2008)
2. Ambler, S.W., Sadalage, P.J.: Refactoring Databases: Evolutionary Database Design. Addison-Wesley Professional, Boston (2006)
3. Cooper, B.F., Silberstein, A., Tam, E., Ramakrishnan, R., Sears, R.: Benchmarking cloud serving systems with YCSB. In: Proceedings of the SoCC 2010. ACM (2010)

4. Curino, C.A., Tanca, L., Moon, H.J., Zaniolo, C.: Schema evolution in wikipedia: toward a web information system benchmark. In: Proceedings of the ICEIS 2008 (2008)

5. Fry, J.P., Sibley, E.H.: Evolution of data-base management systems. ACM Comput. Surv. **8**(1), 7–42 (1976)

6. Ghazal, A., et al.: BigBench: towards an industry standard benchmark for big data analytics. In: Proceedings of the SIGMOD 2013 (2013)

7. Gray, J. (ed.): The Benchmark Handbook for Database and Transaction Systems, 2nd edn. Morgan Kaufmann, Burlington (1993)

8. Han, R., John, L.K., Zhan, J.: Benchmarking big data systems: a review. IEEE Trans. Serv. Comput. **11**(3), 580–597 (2018)

9. Han, R., Lu, X.: On big data benchmarking. CoRR abs/1402.5194 (2014)

10. Herrmann, K., Voigt, H., Behrend, A., Rausch, J., Lehner, W.: Living in parallel realities: co-existing schema versions with a bidirectional database evolution language. In: Proceedings of the SIGMOD 2017 (2017)

11. Hillenbrand, A., Levchenko, M., Störl, U., Scherzinger, S., Klettke, M.: MigCast: putting a price tag on data model evolution in NoSQL data stores. In: Proceedings of the SIGMOD 2019 (2019)

12. Karimov, J., Rabl, T., Markl, V.: PolyBench: the first benchmark for polystores. In: Nambiar, R., Poess, M. (eds.) TPCTC 2018. LNCS, vol. 11135, pp. 24–41. Springer, Cham (2019). https://doi.org/10.1007/978-3-030-11404-6_3

13. Klettke, M., Störl, U., Shenavai, M., Scherzinger, S.: NoSQL schema evolution and big data migration at scale. In: Proceedings of the SCDM 2016 (2016)

14. Lin, D.Y., Neamtiu, I.: Collateral evolution of applications and databases. In: Proceedings of the IWPSE-Evol 2009 (2009)

15. Möller, M.L., Klettke, M., Hillenbrand, A., Störl, U.: Query rewriting for continuously evolving NoSQL databases. In: Laender, A.H.F., Pernici, B., Lim, E.-P., de Oliveira, J.P.M. (eds.) ER 2019. LNCS, vol. 11788, pp. 213–221. Springer, Cham (2019). https://doi.org/10.1007/978-3-030-33223-5_18

16. Qiu, D., Li, B., Su, Z.: An empirical analysis of the co-evolution of schema and code in database applications. In: Proceedings of the ESEC/FSE 2013 (2013)

17. Brueckner, R.: New TPCx-BB Benchmark Compares Big Data Analytics Systems. https://insidehpc.com/2016/06/transaction-processing-performance-council-tpctm-launches-tpcx-bb-a-new-benchmark-for-big-data-analytics-systems/. Accessed 03 Apr 2020

18. Roddick, J.F.: A survey of schema versioning issues for database systems. Inf. Softw. Technol. **37**(7), 383–393 (1995)

19. Saur, K., Dumitraş, T., Hicks, M.: Evolving NoSQL databases without downtime. In: Proceedings of the ICSME 2016 (2016)

20. Scherzinger, S., Klettke, M., Störl, U.: Managing schema evolution in NoSQL data stores. In: Proceedings of the DBPL 2013 (2013)

21. Skoulis, I., Vassiliadis, P., Zarras, A.V.: Growing up with stability. Inf. Syst. **53**(C), 363–385 (2015)

22. Transaction Processing Council: TPC Benchmarks Overview. http://www.tpc.org/information/benchmarks5.asp. Accessed 28 Nov 2019

23. Transaction Processing Council: TPC Express Big Bench, TPCx-BB Standard Specification, Version 1.3.1. http://www.tpc.org/tpc_documents_current_versions/pdf/tpcx-bb_v1.3.1.pdf. Accessed 29 Nov 2019

24. Wang, Y., Dong, J., Shah, R., Dillig, I.: Synthesizing database programs for schema refactoring. In: Proceedings of the PLDI 2019 (2019)

25. Wevers, L., Hofstra, M., Tammens, M., Huisman, M., van Keulen, M.: A benchmark for online non-blocking schema transformations. In: Proceedings of the DATA 2015 (2015)
26. Wu, S., Neamtiu, I.: Schema evolution analysis for embedded databases. In: Proceedings of the ICDEW 2011 (2011)
27. Zhang, C., Lu, J., Xu, P., Chen, Y.: UniBench: a benchmark for multi-model database management Systems. In: Nambiar, R., Poess, M. (eds.) TPCTC 2018. LNCS, vol. 11135, pp. 7–23. Springer, Cham (2019). https://doi.org/10.1007/978-3-030-11404-6_2

Capability Management of Digital Business Ecosystems – A Case of Resilience Modeling in the Healthcare Domain

Chen Hsi Tsai[✉] [iD], Jelena Zdravkovic[iD], and Janis Stirna[iD]

Department of Computer and Systems Sciences, Stockholm University, Stockholm, Sweden
{chenhsi.tsai,jelenaz,js}@dsv.su.se

Abstract. Significant amount of business collaboration takes place online which supports efficient and dynamic business partnerships. Once such partnerships reach a critical mass, a digital business ecosystem (DBE) forms. While it is beneficial to its actors, it is also complex and more difficult to manage. A key management concern is resilience, especially in the context of digitalization. The relevant goals influencing the DBE resilience are diversity, efficiency, adaptability, and cohesion, which need to be aligned with business goals of a specific DBE and managed accordingly. To this end, the paper investigates the suitability of capability management for the purpose of analyzing DBEs to support resilience and demonstrates capability models for a digital health use case in the healthcare sector.

Keywords: Digital business ecosystem · Capability management · Enterprise Modeling · Resilience

1 Introduction

Increased competition in business drives organizations to take a more collaborative approach by joining forces and partnering with other organizations/entities to combine expertise and capabilities as a way to attain resilience and agility. Given the opportunity provided by the advancement of information and communications technologies, much of collaboration happens online which fosters efficiency and allows easy entrance of new partners. This, in essence leads, to forming a *digital business ecosystem* (DBE).

A *digital business ecosystem* (DBE), based on Moore's concept of *business ecosystem* [1, 2], emerge as an environment where coevolution of interconnecting organizations and individuals can be facilitated by information and communications technologies [3]. For various organizations, DBE presents a novel approach to leverage resources across multiple actors and even different industries to meet elaborate needs of customers [4].

A more collaborative approach with DBE brings also enhanced complexity of interactions, interconnections, and interrelationships among involving actors such as partners and customers. Unforeseen events or business decisions and actions taken by one actor can influence all interrelated actors in the DBE. Such complexity in a DBE can make it

© Springer Nature Switzerland AG 2020
N. Herbaut and M. La Rosa (Eds.): CAiSE Forum 2020, LNBIP 386, pp. 126–137, 2020.
https://doi.org/10.1007/978-3-030-58135-0_11

difficult to manage the whole ecosystem real-time due to partial information provided by individual actors or suppliers.

The state of the art in DBE design and management suggests that these tasks are not approached holistically. Much of the current efforts are devoted to analysis. The current efforts in methodologies for DBE, e.g. for analysis and modeling [5–9], actor visualization [7], DBE related ontologies [10, 11], offer only partial solutions. There is no methodological guidance for a holistic way of analyzing, designing, and managing complex systems or ecosystems from a multi-actor perspective. Neither is there a focus nor adequate research on using models for management purposes, specifically for managing resilience, in such complex ecosystems as DBEs. A key aspect of managing resilient DBEs is the need to oversee which actors exist, what they do and the dynamics, and what changes depending on the situation at hand. On a level of a single organization or an organization in customer-supplier situation this has been addressed by Capability Management [12]. Hence, a working hypothesis explored in this paper is the suitability of capability management for addressing DBEs. In this light, objectives of this study are: (1) to investigate the suitability of capability management for management of DBEs in order to support resilience, and (2) to discuss a digital health use case in the healthcare sector from the point of view of capability management.

The rest of the paper is structured in the following way. Section 2 gives background to ecosystem, business ecosystem, and DBE. Section 3 presents the theoretical proposal of resilience and management of DBE with a capability focus. Section 4 elaborated the theoretical proposal with an approach applied to an industrial case. A discussion and concluding remarks are presented in Sect. 5.

2 Background

'Ecosystem' is a term that has been used in biology for long. According to the online Oxford English Dictionary, an ecosystem is defined as: "a biological system composed of all the organisms found in a particular physical environment, interacting with it and with each other. Also, in extended use: a complex system resembling this."

In recent years, the concept of ecosystem has gained awareness and significance in many fields including information systems (IS). In the following, some extended uses of 'ecosystem' related to this study and the IS discipline are explained.

Moore, in 1993, suggested a new idea of cooperative networks which resembles an ecological ecosystem: a *business ecosystem* [1]. A *business ecosystem* bears similarity to an ecological ecosystem as being a complex system involving evolution and co-evolution [1]. Later in 1996, the concept of '*business ecosystem*' was further defined by Moore [2] as: "an economic community supported by a foundation of interacting organizations and individuals– 'the organisms of the business world'."

Various actors, suppliers, competitors, and others, exist in the ecosystem. Customers, as members of the ecosystem, consume goods and services produced by the economic community. With time, co-evolution occurs in the *business ecosystem*, i.e. organizations and individuals co-evolve roles and capabilities. They are inclined to align with the outlook set by "central companies" holding leadership roles. Similar to evolution in ecological ecosystems, entities having leadership roles in a *business ecosystem* may also change and evolve with time, but the function of a leader remains the same.

Since Moore applied the concept of ecological ecosystem to business and strategy, several IS engineering-related applications have emerged such as *digital ecosystem* and *digital business ecosystem* that are described in the next paragraphs.

Briscoe and De Wilde extended a Service-Oriented Architecture with Distributed Evolutionary Computing and proposed a new distributed optimization architecture: a *digital ecosystem* [13]. They argued that this was the first interpretation of a *digital ecosystem* that was more than a metaphor since the proposed architecture possesses some of the properties of an ecological ecosystem, such as robustness, self-organization, scalability, and sustainability. It also demonstrates emergent behaviors as observed in complex systems, such as being able to provide software services more than the constituent parts could offer.

The *digital ecosystem* architecture incorporated a twofold optimization process as part of the innovative form of distributed evolutionary computing. This enhanced the capability of solving more dynamic and complex problem through evolution of software services in the ecosystem by searching and forming new algorithms automatically in the scalable architecture.

The concept of *digital business ecosystem* was introduced, based on Moore's *business ecosystem* [2], in the Directorate General Information Society of the European Commission [14]. After the launch of the European Union Framework VI Information Society Technologies project Digital Business Ecosystems (grant ID 507953), the concept has been further defined and started to be widely used [3].

A DBE highlights the coevolution between the business aspect and its partial digital representation in the ecosystem [3]. It emerges as an environment, aiming for evolution, self-organization, and self-optimization, where interconnecting organizations and individuals in an economic community coevolve their capabilities and roles by means of information and communications technologies [3]. As a biological metaphor emphasizing the interdependent actors in the ecosystem, the digital aspect of DBE considers a technical infrastructure distributing any useful digital representations, such as software applications, services, descriptions of skills, laws, etc., while the business aspect is similar to Moore's idea [2].

2.1 Current State of Digital Business Ecosystems

An ongoing systematic literature review investigating the current scientific knowledge in DBEs indicated that most efforts focused on analysis and design. Several studies proposed methodologies or frameworks for DBE analysis and modeling [5–7] such as BEAM [8] and MOBENA [9]. Modeling language were developed or further specified to support analysis and design of DBE [15, 16]. Furthermore, attempts to depict DBE actors and their relations with visual languages or visualizations were made [7]. MAS2DES-Onto and other DBE related ontologies were also developed [10, 11]. Methodologies for designing DBE were suggested [17]. Also, studies with focus on DBE architecture were conducted [18, 19].

Of few studies focused on DBE management, a framework for DBE integration based on the Zachman framework was proposed [20]. Another study suggested management of DBE using performance measures such as innovation, contribution, prestige, and resilience indicators [21].

To our knowledge, management of DBE has not yet been investigated in depth and published in the scientific literature. In this paper, we went beyond the state of the art and addressed DBE management with a focus in resilience.

3 Positioning Resilience for Digital Business Ecosystems

Given the gap in the knowledge of resilience for DBE, we proposed the idea with a capability focus for management and monitoring of DBE in the interest of supporting resilience.

Despite the initial introduction of the concept 'resilience' in ecology [22], much research has been undertaken on resilience in several disciplines, including IS engineering and other engineering fields. Resilience is often defined as *the ability to remain or recover to a stable state to continuously operate during and after a crucial mishap or under constant stress* [23].

As in an ecological ecosystem, through coevolution and evolution among the great number of species the nature has its way of remaining and recovering to a stable state. Concerning DBE, resilience, as a built-in concept, resembles the nature's way since a DBE is, by definition, a metaphor of an ecological ecosystem. Hence, the abundance of species/actors, the interconnections among these species/actors, and the coevolution and evolution among them are some factors of the key to resilience in not only an ecological ecosystem but also a DBE. This leads us to the core of positioning resilience in a DBE for the purpose of this study: to monitor coevolution and evolution of the actors during and after context changes in a DBE. This is to be seen in conjunction with a number of overarching DBE resilience goals. Taking inspiration from [24], they consist of *diversity, efficiency, adaptability,* and *cohesion*. Diversity means the variety of actors for organizational units and roles in a DBE, the collection of multiple resources and resource variety in a DBE, and the collection of multiple capabilities and capabilities variety in a DBE. Efficiency concerns resource productivity and utilization in a DBE and value delivered relative to total resource consumption. Adaptability denotes transparency in terms of exposing the means of adaptation and flexibility as the ease with which a DBE can be changed. Expressing DBE design in terms of capabilities, key performance indicators, context data contributes to DBE's adaptability. Cohesion represents strong partnerships, the alignment and tightness among actors and their capabilities, towards fulfilling the mission of a DBE.

While equilibrium and survival may be the consistent and ultimate goals related to resilience for all species as a whole in ecological ecosystems, DBEs may have different domain specific DBE resilience goals and business goals. These goals are often set by central actors holding the leadership or regulatory roles. By continuously fulfilling these goals, a DBE achieves resilience.

4 Digital Health Platform: A Digital Business Ecosystem

Applying the theoretical proposal of resilience modeling to the case of the digital health DBE, we adopted the following procedure: (1) identify actors and resources using 4EM method; (2) extract and match the three levels of goals; (3) document DBE capabilities and their relations in capability maps; and (4) depict the capability constellation with descriptions of KPIs and contexts aligning with DBE business goals. The next steps needed to be carried out would be documenting capability designs for the specific capabilities and modeling relevant context elements and measurable properties, which represent data entities for DBE monitoring. Additionally, once all actors of the DBE are analyzed, the conflicts between their business goals and the DBE level goals might need to be resolved, e.g. the actors' interest to expand versus the DBE goals to retain actor diversity.

The digital health platform case used as an example for this study is a European Institute of Innovation and Technology Health (EIT Health) Innovation by Design project [25]. The purpose of the example case is to demonstrate our attempt to model and monitor DBE resilience with capability management. From the point of view of resilience monitoring, an outbreak of a contagious disease is considered the stressful condition/changing context of which the digital health DBE is facing.

The digital health DBE consists of actors such as digital and physical health service providers, health product suppliers, digital health platform company, private employers and their employees as individual users, public sectors, and investors. The digital health platform company, as one of the central actors holding the leadership role in the DBE, owns a digital health platform. The aim of the company is to shift the focus in healthcare from reactive to proactive by providing tailored services based on personal needs and supporting healthier lifestyle habits through the digital platform. Also, a health outcomes-based contracting model is investigated by the digital health platform company, public sectors, and investors. Figure 1 depicts actors and resources for this case in the form of 4EM [26] Actors and Resources Model.

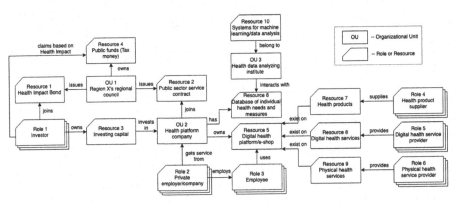

Fig. 1. Actor-resource 4EM model of the digital health DBE.

The user's journey began with filling out a health and lifestyle questionnaire, taking a blood sample and a set of physical measurements. The information was analyzed by professionals and the health data analyzing institute. Later, the analyzed report was reviewed by the user together with a personal health coach in order to tailor a health plan with timed goals based on personal needs, preferences, and conditions. The user then received a balance which can be spent on the digital health platform populated by various health services and products to turn the plan into actions. When the cycle of the user's health plan ended, measurements were taken based on the set goals. The measurement data was then analyzed by the health data analyzing institute to see if the expected health outcome had been achieved. The analysis was also used by the digital health platform company to improve effectiveness of services.

In the digital health case example, the digital health platform company is considered as one of the central companies in the DBE. Therefore, the DBE resilience goals (cf. Sect. 3) are concretized as Domain Specific DBE resilience goals for the healthcare domain together with the DBE business goals based on the viewpoint of the digital health platform company in Table 1.

Table 1. Resilience and business goals for the digital health DBE

Resilience goal	Domain specific resilience goal	Business goal
Diversity	To ensure different health services, health products, and health information are accessible and usable by different groups of actors in the healthcare DBE	To provide the right health products on digital health platform
		To make the right digital health services offered on digital health platform
		To make the right physical health services offered on digital health platform
Efficiency	To improve health conditions of clients with optimal amount of accessible resources in the healthcare DBE	To tailor health plan by planning efficient and effective health activities with needed resources
Adaptability	To ensure flexibility of health services and products based on context changes in the healthcare DBE	To tailor health plan based on personal preferences and lifestyles
Cohesion	To ensure all stakeholders in the healthcare DBE adhere to policy and care plan during care process	To promote proactive healthcare complied with public regulations
		To increase individual users' compliance to the healthy lifestyle supported by digital health platform

Based on Fig. 1, a capability map is created for OU1 region X's regional council, OU2 digital health platform company, OU3 health data analyzing institute, Role1 investor, Role4 health product supplier, Role5 digital health service provider, and Role6 physical health service provider (Fig. 2). Taking a capability of the digital health platform company as example, capability 4.1 Digital health platform contains two sub-capabilities - 4.1.1 IT infrastructure and 4.1.2 System maintenance.

Figure 3 further elaborates the supporting relations among capabilities in the DBE using the example of five capabilities (4.1, 4.2, 4.3, 4.4, and 4.7) and two sub-capabilities

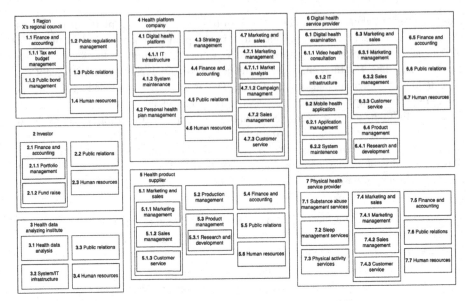

Fig. 2. Capability map of the digital health DBE

(4.7.1 and 4.7.1.1) from the viewpoint of the digital health platform company. The color coding of the arrows is matched with the colors assigned to each actor.

On the basis of Fig. 3, a capability interface constellation [27], addressing capability 4.1 and 4.2 of the digital health platform company, depicts the supporting relations together with the key performance indicators (KPIs) and the context sets as shown in Fig. 4. In this process, KPIs and context sets are identified, to be used for capability monitoring purposes. Due to the lack of space, this paper omits specifying from what measurable properties and context elements the KPIs and context sets are calculated, which would have to be done to make the capability management operational. Cf. [12] for more details on this topic. The KPIs and context sets are mapped with the DBE business goals in Table 2 in order to be used for monitoring and supporting resilience of the digital health DBE.

Considering an outbreak of a contagious disease (the stressful condition/changing context for the DBE), people's lifestyle choices, working conditions, and preferences may change in order to prevent from being infected. Individual users who used to prefer attending yoga sessions physically may wish to alter their health plans and attend online sessions through mobile applications instead. As shown in Table 2, by monitoring KPI 4.1, we could observe if the number of yoga sessions taken physically by individual users complying with health plans has dropped; with KPI 4.2, we could observe the change in the number of physical and online yoga sessions in health plans supported by the digital health platform; with KPI 5.2, we could observe the change in number of supplied product for yoga and if it is adequate; and with KPI 6.2, we could see if the number of mobile application for yoga on the digital health platform is sufficient. Based on these observations of KPIs, changes could be made for the situation, in this case an epidemic causing users' preference changes. Through monitoring and making

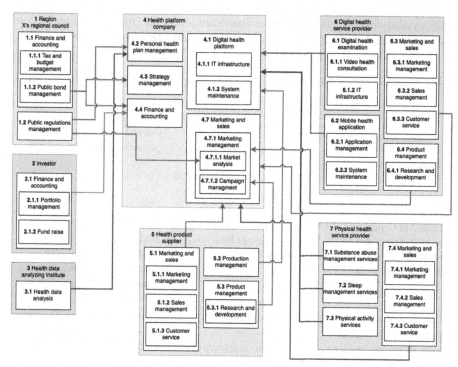

Fig. 3. Digital health platform company's capabilities and the supporting capabilities from other actors in DBE

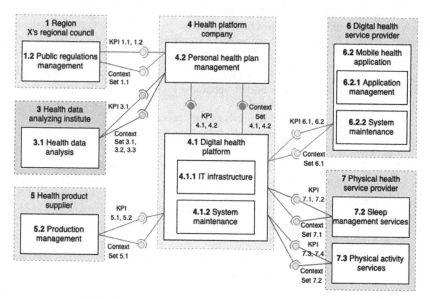

Fig. 4. Capability interfaces for the digital health DBE

capability adjustments accordingly under a persistent stress, the DBE gains better support in striving to fulfills its business goals and could more likely achieve resilience.

Table 2. Business goals, KPIs, and context sets of the capabilities or the digital health DBE

Business goal	Key performance indicator	Context set
To promote proactive healthcare complied with public regulations	KPI 1.1: number of types of permitted proactive health interventions KPI 1.2: number of permitted proactive health interventions per type	Context set 1.1: current policies and public regulations
To tailor health plan by planning efficient and effective health activities with needed resources	KPI 3.1: effectiveness of health measures based on timed health plan goals	Context set 3.1: actual health guidelines Context set 3.2: effective models of health measures Context set 3.3: age, medical history, etc.
To increase individual users' compliance to the healthy lifestyle supported by digital health platform	KPI 4.1: number of used health measures (product/service) complied with health plan	Context set 4.1: real time data on individual users' usage of health measures (product/service)
To tailor health plan based on personal preferences and lifestyles	KPI 4.2: number of permitted health interventions in health plan supported by digital health platform per type	Context set 4.2: currently permitted health interventions in health plan
To provide the right health products on digital health platform	KPI 5.1: number of types of supplied health products KPI 5.2: number of supplied health products per type	Context set 5.1: current product details and catalogue
To make the right digital health services offered on digital health platform	KPI 6.1: number of types of mobile health applications developed KPI 6.2: number of developed mobile health applications per type	Context set 6.1: current mobile health applications
To make the right physical health services offered on digital health platform	KPI 7.1: number of types of sleep-management services available KPI 7.2: number of available sleep-management services per type	Context set 7.1: currently available sleep-management services

(continued)

Table 2. (*continued*)

Business goal	Key performance indicator	Context set
	KPI 7.3: number of types of physical activity services available KPI 7.4: number of available physical activity services per type	Context set 7.2: currently available physical activity services

5   Conclusions and Future Work

This paper has applied the principles of DBE thinking and capability management to a use case on digital health. The use case is based on a variety of actors delivering capabilities to each other as well as to individual customers. The main focus of this study has been the consideration of multifactor constellations in terms of the principles of ecosystem; and a structured (model-based) elaboration of the concept of DBE resilience. Concerning the objectives of the paper a number of reflections can be made.

In terms of the suitability of capability management, the approach used in this paper includes Enterprise Modeling, hence it allows dealing with various levels of goals and capabilities as well as concepts needed for their management (KPIs and context). These aspects are currently underdeveloped in the state-of-the-art contributions for DBE analysis from literature.

Concerning modeling the case of the digital health DBE, Enterprise Modeling and capability modeling supported the identification of actors and their relationships. Modelling goals and KPIs from the perspectives of resilience led to considerations of means for monitoring and management. For the DBE as a whole, the modelling effort helped knowledge explication, which increased transparency of the DBE. In this regard, we consider that it contributed to the adaptability of the DBE. This can be further increased by creating a capability repository, which would also reduce the entry barriers of health product suppliers, digital health service providers, and physical health service providers. The concept of capability is used in the enterprise architecture management frameworks (see summary in [28]), hence it would be deemed familiar to many companies.

A few limitations remain in this paper. Firstly, how the capability map was defined in the case was not fully reported since collecting capabilities into a capability map could be seen as a common practice. Secondly, how KPIs and context sets are calculated based on measurable properties and context elements was not thoroughly considered in this paper due to the limited space and the limited information obtained from the case. Lastly, the context that we addressed in this paper is based on the state of the art in context modeling and management [12]. Considering the social perspective, especially the cultural and legal contexts, it would be important to know what these contexts are in measurable terms and how to incorporate them in the context platform in order to address them properly.

Future work will focus on the automation of context dependent adjustment of the DBE; modeling of goals of the DBE at different levels; compliance monitoring, as well as monitoring and management of capabilities of the actors from the point of view of resilience.

References

1. Moore, J.F.: Predators and prey: a new ecology of competition. Harvard Bus. Rev. **71**(3), 75–86 (1993)
2. Moore, J.F.: The Death of Competition: Leadership and Strategy in the Age of Business Ecosystems. Harper Business, New York (1996)
3. Nachira, F., Dini, P., Nicolai, A.: A network of digital business ecosystems for Europe: roots, processes and perspectives. In: Nachira, F., Nicolai, A., Dini, P., Le Louarn, M., Rivera Leon, L. (eds.) Digital Business Ecosystems. European Commission, Bruxelles (2007)
4. Senyo, P.K., Liu, K., Effah, J.: Digital business ecosystem: literature review and a framework for future research. Int. J. Inf. Manage. **47**, 52–64 (2019)
5. Boffoli, N., Cimitile, M., Maggi, F.M., Visaggio, G.: An approach to digital business ecosystems based on process models. In: D'Atri, A., De Marco, M., Braccini, A., Cabiddu, F. (eds.) Management of the Interconnected World, pp. 511–518. Physica-Verlag HD, Heidelberg (2010). https://doi.org/10.1007/978-3-7908-2404-9_59
6. Aldea, A., Kusumaningrum, M.C., Iacob, M.E., Daneva, M.: Modeling and analyzing digital business ecosystems: an approach and evaluation. In: 20th IEEE International Conference on Business Informatics CBI 2018, pp. 156–163. Institute of Electrical and Electronics Engineers Inc. (2018)
7. Faber, A., Rehm, S.V., Hernandez-Mendez, A., Matthes, F.: Modeling and visualizing smart city mobility business ecosystems: insights from a case study. Information **9**(11), 270 (2018)
8. Tian, C.H., Ray, B.K., Lee, J., Cao, R., Ding, W.: BEAM: a framework for business ecosystem analysis and modeling. IBM Syst. J. **47**(1), 101–114 (2008)
9. Battistella, C., Colucci, K., De Toni, A.F., Nonino, F.: Methodology of business ecosystems network analysis: a case study in Telecom Italia Future Centre. Technol. Forecast. Soc. Chang. **80**(6), 1194–1210 (2013)
10. Cojocaru, L.-E., Sarraipa, J., Jardim-Golcalves, R., Stanescu, A.M.: Digital business ecosystem framework for the agro-food industry. In: Mertins, K., Bénaben, F., Poler, R., Bourrières, J.-P. (eds.) Enterprise Interoperability VI. PIC, vol. 7, pp. 285–296. Springer, Cham (2014). https://doi.org/10.1007/978-3-319-04948-9_24
11. Kidanu, S.A., Chbeir, R., Cardinale, Y.: MAS2DES-onto: ontology for MAS-based digital ecosystems. In: 43rd Latin American Computer Conference CLEI 2017, pp. 1–8. Institute of Electrical and Electronics Engineers Inc. (2017)
12. Sandkuhl, K., Stirna, J. (eds.): Capability Management in Digital Enterprises. Springer, Cham (2018). https://doi.org/10.1007/978-3-319-90424-5
13. Briscoe, G., De Wilde, P.: Digital ecosystems: evolving service-orientated architectures. In: Proceedings of the 1st International Conference on Bio Inspired Models of Network, Information and Computing Systems, pp. 17–es. Association for Computing Machinery (2006)
14. Nachira, F.: Toward a Network of Digital Business Ecosystems Fostering the Local Development. European Commission, Bruxelles (2002)
15. Ferronato, P.: A business modelling language (BML) for digital business ecosystem: the DBE project case. In: 2006 IEEE International Technology Management Conference (ICE), pp. 1–10. Institute of Electrical and Electronics Engineers Inc. (2006)
16. Pittl, B., Bork, D.: Modeling digital enterprise ecosystems with ArchiMate: a mobility provision case study. Enterprise Interoperability VI. LNCS, vol. 7, pp. 178–189. Springer, Cham (2017). https://doi.org/10.1007/978-3-319-61240-9_17

17. Hadzic, M., Chang, E.: Application of digital ecosystem design methodology within the health domain. IEEE Trans. Syst. Man Cybern. Part A Syst. Hum. **40**(4), 779–788 (2010)
18. Vasilățeanu, A., Șerbănați, L.D.: Towards an agent-oriented architecture of the digital healthcare ecosystem. UPB Sci. Bull. **74**, 87–102 (2012)
19. Wieringa, R., Engelsman, W., Gordijn, J., Ionita, D.: A business ecosystem architecture modeling framework. In: 21st IEEE Conference on Business Informatics CBI 2019, pp. 147–156. Institute of Electrical and Electronics Engineers Inc. (2019)
20. Korpela, K., Kuusiholma, U., Taipale, O., Hallikas, J.: A framework for exploring digital business ecosystems. In: 46th Annual Hawaii International Conference on System Sciences HICSS 2013, pp. 3838–3847. Institute of Electrical and Electronics Engineers Inc. (2013)
21. Graça, P., Camarinha-Matos, L.M.: A proposal of performance indicators for collaborative business ecosystems. In: Afsarmanesh, H., Camarinha-Matos, L.M., Lucas Soares, A. (eds.) PRO-VE 2016. IAICT, vol. 480, pp. 253–264. Springer, Cham (2016). https://doi.org/10. 1007/978-3-319-45390-3_22
22. Holling, C.S.: Resilience and stability of ecological systems. Annu. Rev. Ecol. Syst. **4**, 1–23 (1973)
23. Wreathall, J.: Properties of resilient organizations: an initial view. In: Hollnagel, E., Woods, D.D., Leveson, N. (eds.) Resilience Engineering: Concepts and Precepts, pp. 275–285. Ashgate Publishing Limited, Aldershot (2006)
24. Fiksel, J.: Designing resilient, sustainable systems. Environ. Sci. Technol. **37**(23), 5330–5339 (2003)
25. EIT Health. https://eithealth.eu/project/the-health-movement/. Accessed 10 Apr 2020
26. Sandkuhl, K., Stirna, J., Persson, A., Wißotzki, M.: Enterprise Modeling. Springer, Heidelberg (2014). https://doi.org/10.1007/978-3-319-94857-7
27. Zdravkovic, J., Stirna, J.: Towards data-driven capability interface. IFAC-PapersOnLine **52**(13), 1126–1131 (2019)
28. Zdravkovic, J., Stirna, J., Grabis, J.: A comparative analysis of using the capability notion for congruent business and information systems engineering. Complex Syst. Inf. Model. Q. **10**, 1–20 (2017)

TOSCA Lightning: An Integrated Toolchain for Transforming TOSCA Light into Production-Ready Deployment Technologies

Michael Wurster[1][✉], Uwe Breitenbücher[1], Lukas Harzenetter[1], Frank Leymann[1], and Jacopo Soldani[2]

[1] Institute of Architecture of Application Systems, University of Stuttgart, Stuttgart, Germany
{wurster,breitenbuecher,harzenetter,leymann}@iaas.uni-stuttgart.de
[2] Department of Computer Science, University of Pisa, Pisa, Italy
soldani@di.unipi.it

Abstract. The OASIS standard TOSCA provides a portable means for specifying multi-service applications and automating their deployment. Despite TOSCA is widely used in research, it is currently not supported by the production-ready deployment technologies daily used by practitioners, hence resulting in a gap between the state-of-the-art in research and the state-of-practice in industry. To help bridging this gap, we identified *TOSCA Light*, a subset of TOSCA enabling the transformation of compliant deployment models to the vast majority of deployment technology-specific models used by practitioners nowadays. In this paper, we demonstrate TOSCA Lightning by two contributions. We (i) present an integrated toolchain for specifying multi-service applications with TOSCA Light and transforming them into different production-ready deployment technologies. Additionally, we (ii) demonstrate the toolchain's effectiveness based on a third-party application and Kubernetes.

Keywords: Deployment automation · Cloud computing · TOSCA · Kubernetes

1 Introduction

Automating the deployment of multi-service applications is crucial, as manually deploying them is time-consuming and error-prone, and since modern software engineering practices (e.g., continuous development and continuous integration) heavily rely on deployment automation [19]. To accomplish this need, various deployment automation technologies have been proposed. Each technology is however typically equipped with its own language for specifying the target deployment for a multi-service application. Such languages either *declaratively*

© Springer Nature Switzerland AG 2020
N. Herbaut and M. La Rosa (Eds.): CAiSE Forum 2020, LNBIP 386, pp. 138–146, 2020.
https://doi.org/10.1007/978-3-030-58135-0_12

describe the desired application configuration or *imperatively* list the technical tasks to be executed to deploy and configure the application [10]. Even if declarative languages are by far considered to be the most appropriate in practice [19], they are tightly coupled to the corresponding deployment technology, hence limiting the portability of application deployments from one technology to another.

In contrast, the *Topology and Orchestration Specification for Cloud Applications* [16] (TOSCA) is a standardized modeling language allowing to declaratively specify portable multi-service application deployments. While it is heavily used in research [1], TOSCA is currently not supported by the production-ready deployment technologies daily used by practitioners. As a result, a gap between the academic state-of-the-art and the industrial state-of-practice is arising.

To help bridging this gap, we identified the *TOSCA Light* [20] subset of TOSCA, which can be automatically transformed to the vast majority of deployment technology-specific languages. TOSCA Light identifies the subset of TOSCA that complies with the *Essential Deployment Metamodel* (EDMM), a set of core deployment modeling entities that the 13 most used deployment technologies understand [19]. Any deployment modeling language relying on the entities of EDMM can hence be converted to multiple heterogeneous technology-specific deployment artifacts [18]. TOSCA Light is exactly that subset of the TOSCA specification that complies with EDMM and, thus, multi-service application deployments written in TOSCA Light can be processed to obtain technology-specific deployment models, including required artifacts and templates [20].

Our objective in this paper is to demonstrate the potentials and practical applicability of this approach by introducing the *TOSCA Lightning* toolchain and to show how TOSCA Light favors the portability of multi-service application deployments. We show that TOSCA Light enhances the portability of deployment models as it can be used for devising technology-agnostic specifications that can be translated to different technology-specific deployment artifacts. With TOSCA Light, application developers can indeed specify their application deployment only once, still being able to actually deploy the specified application on multiple production-ready deployment technologies such as Kubernetes or Terraform.

In this perspective, the contribution of this demonstrator paper is twofold. We first present (i) the open-source TOSCA Lightning integrated toolchain. TOSCA Lightning enables specifying multi-service applications in TOSCA validating their compliance with TOSCA Light and generating the technology-specific artifacts for actually enacting their deployment on production-ready deployment technologies. Moreover, we present (ii) an end-to-end case study based on a third-party application. The case study illustrates how to exploit the TOSCA Lightning toolchain to validly specify the application with TOSCA Light and to automatically generate the artifacts for actually deploying the application with one of the supported production-ready technologies, e.g., Kubernetes.

In the following, Sect. 2 presents the integrated *TOSCA Lightning* toolchain and Sect. 3 shows its application to a concrete case study. Section 4 and Sect. 5 discuss related work and draw some concluding remarks, respectively.

2 The TOSCA Lightning Toolchain

We hereby introduce all components forming the integrated *TOSCA Lightning* toolchain and explain the user's workflow. The toolchain consists of four components in total, as depicted in Fig. 1. Two of them were newly developed within the scope of this paper, namely the *TOSCA Lightning User Interface* and the *TOSCA Lightning API*. Further, two existing components, namely Eclipse Winery [15] and the EDMM Transformation Framework [18], were integrated into the proposed toolchain by utilizing their corresponding APIs. The TOSCA Lightning toolchain is *open source* and available on GitHub[1], including a demonstration video.

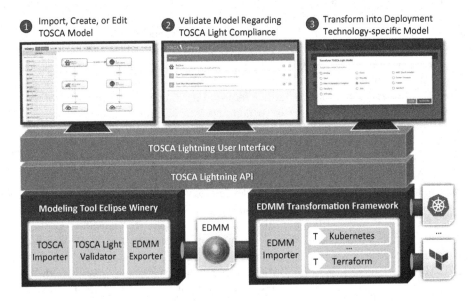

Fig. 1. The TOSCA Lightning toolchain (new integration components colored green). (Color figure online)

In the scope of this paper, we developed the TOSCA Lightning User Interface and the TOSCA Lightning API to fully integrate the TOSCA modeling tool Eclipse Winery and the EDMM Transformation Framework to enable transformation. The TOSCA Lightning User Interface is the user's main entry point and acts as a dashboard to list, create, change, or transform compliant TOSCA

---

[1] https://github.com/UST-EDMM/tosca-lightning.

Light models. The TOSCA Lightning API respectively encapsulates the REST APIs over HTTP of Eclipse Winery and the EDMM Transformation Framework to provide a uniform interface for the integrated TOSCA Lightning toolchain.

The TOSCA Lightning User Interface is able to launch the modeling environment Eclipse Winery [15] to import, create, or edit TOSCA Light models. Eclipse Winery is a web-based environment to graphically model TOSCA-based application topologies and provides a *Management Interface* to manage all TOSCA related entities, such as node types, their property definitions, operations, and artifacts. Further, it provides a *Topology Modeler* component which enables the graphical composition of an application and its desired target state. Winery has been extended by various features, which can be enabled by so-called *feature flags*, to provide the necessary TOSCA Light capabilities, e.g., to validate whether imported or created TOSCA models are compliant with TOSCA Light.

The TOSCA Lightning User Interface enables users to execute the transformation of a TOSCA Light model into a *deployment technology-specific model* (DTSM) by selecting one of the supported deployment technologies. For this transformation, the user interface invokes via the TOSCA Lightning API the Eclipse Winery API to export the selected TOSCA Light model as EDMM model, which can be processed afterward by the EDMM Transformation Framework [18]. Exporting TOSCA Light models as EDMM models is possible since TOSCA Light can be directly mapped to EDMM [19,20]. Thus, the EDMM Transformation Framework enables transforming a given EDMM model into required artifacts, i.e., files and models, to execute the deployment using the selected deployment technology's tooling. The EDMM Transformation Framework is plugin-based and, at the time of writing, supports via the EDMM Transformation Framework the transformation into DTSMs of 13 deployment automation technologies, such as Kubernetes, Terraform, Chef, Puppet, and AWS CloudFormation. We hereafter illustrate how users work with the TOSCA Lightning toolchain:

Import, Create, or Edit TOSCA Model. Eclipse Winery provides the *TOSCA Importer* functionality to easily reuse and adapt existing TOSCA deployment models. Users can create new models or edit existing models by graphically composing the component structure of the desired application. The application's component structure is indeed described declaratively using TOSCA modeling constructs. The resulting model comprises all TOSCA-based definitions and entities describing types, component instances, their properties, operations, and file artifacts required for deploying and operating the application.

Validate Model Regarding TOSCA Light Compliance. The validation of the TOSCA model is performed at *design time* using the *TOSCA Light Validator* component of Eclipse Winery. It checks the TOSCA Light compliance of imported or created TOSCA deployment models. The models are checked against a set of TOSCA Light modeling requirements [20]. In case the model is compliant with TOSCA Light, it is shown in the TOSCA Lightning User Interface. In situations where the model is not compatible with TOSCA Light, the model can be refined according to the provided modification recommendations, presented to the user as a list of violated conditions inside Eclipse Winery.

Transform into DTSM. TOSCA Lightning is able to transform a validated TOSCA Light model into a DTSM by integrating Eclipse Winery and the EDMM Transformation Framework. The model exchange between Eclipse Winery and EDMM Transformation Framework is realized by file transfer, as depicted in Fig. 1. Eclipse Winery's *EDMM Exporter* component produces the output according to the *input file* specifications of the EDMM Transformation Framework. Thus, the output can be directly used for transforming the model into the desired target deployment model format. Notably, the possibility to transform the model is guaranteed by design since the used modeling constructs conform to the essential entities defined by EDMM and, thus, are compliant with TOSCA Light. Users simply select one of the 13 supported deployment automation technologies (e.g., Kubernetes) for the TOSCA Light model that should be transformed. Afterward, users can download the transformation result containing the respective files and templates generated by the EDMM Transformation Framework. At this stage, the generated target deployment model is ready to be deployed using the target technology's tooling. Hence, the actual deployment happens using the actual tools and mechanisms provided by the target deployment automation technology.

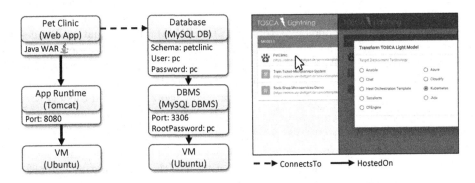

Fig. 2. Case study: transforming TOSCA Light to Kubernetes.

3   Case Study: Transforming TOSCA Light to Kubernetes

Today, Kubernetes is one of the fastest-growing open-source projects. Gartner predicts that by 2022, more than 75% of global enterprises will be using containerized applications in production, and Kubernetes will play an important role [8]. Therefore, we want to show how a declaratively modeled TOSCA Light application can be deployed to Kubernetes by generating the required files and template to execute the deployment on a running Kubernetes cluster.

For the sake of demonstration, we prepared a TOSCA deployment model of the Spring PetClinic application that demonstrates the use of the Spring framework (fork of Java's Pet Store application), which represents a simple software for a veterinary clinic. It is a well-known demo web application running on a Tomcat web server while connecting to a MySQL database to store its data. The respective TOSCA model is schematically depicted on the left-hand side in Fig. 2. For reasons of space limitations, we hereby only show the deployment of the depicted PetClinic application to Kubernetes. However, its deployment can be achieved with any of the other 12 deployment automation technologies or any other TOSCA deployment model supported by the TOSCA Lightning toolchain.

The application model is created or imported using Eclipse Winery. The model itself is not specifically composed for Kubernetes as the target runtime environment. Instead, it is modeled in a generic, component-based manner that will be later translated into the respective files and templates required by Kubernetes, e.g., Dockerfiles, Kubernets Deployment, and Kubernetes Service descriptors. The TOSCA Lightning User Interface lists all available TOSCA Light compliant service templates after it has been started with Docker[2].

Users can open the Topology Editor to display the application's component structure. Further, the Topology Editor is used to set property values which will be used as configuration for instantiating the components at runtime. Eclipse Winery in our demonstration scenario already comes with a set of built-in modeling types, which can be used to model new applications. However, these types follow the proposed normative types by the TOSCA Simple Profile standard [16], while new types can be imported or added manually using Eclipse Winery.

The TOSCA Lightning User Interface and its way to select a transformation target for a certain model is depicted on the right-hand side in Fig. 2. Users can transform the PetClinic application to Kubernetes by selecting the respective entry in the pop-up dialog. The Kubernetes plugin of the EDMM Transformation Framework tries to identify component stacks, a set of tightly coupled components, i.e., components related with "HostedOn" relations. Further, the plugin produces a Dockerfile as well as a Kubernetes Deployment and Kubernetes Service for each component stack. Once the transformation has been performed, users can download the transformation result. From here, users can now use the technology's native tooling, i.e., use Docker and its tooling to build the Docker images based on the translated Dockerfiles and the `kubectl` command-line tool to "apply" the produced Kubernetes descriptor files to a cluster. An in-depth step by step guide as well as a video[3] demonstrating the execution of the Kubernetes deployment is available online and part of our GitHub repository.

---

[2] A Docker Compose file to start the TOSCA Lightning toolchain, a demonstration video, an in-depth quickstart guide, and ready-to-use TOSCA models are available in our GitHub repository: https://ust-edmm.github.io/tosca-lightning.

[3] https://github.com/UST-EDMM/tosca-lightning#video.

4   Related Work

The closest approach to ours is that by Brabra et al. [2], which exploits model-to-model and model-to-text transformations to obtain artifacts for deploying a TOSCA application with four production-ready deployment technologies. Similarly to our approach, Brabra et al. [2] identifies a subset of TOSCA that can be processed by restricting inter-component relationships to *horizontal* dependencies (indicating that a component connects to/depends on another), in order to generate the deployment artifacts for Docker, Juju, Kubernetes, or Terraform. Our solution can deal with a wider set of application topologies, as it also includes *vertical* dependencies (indicating that a component is installed/hosted on another), and it already targets nine more deployment technologies in addition to those targeted by Brabra et al. [2].

Other approaches are aiming at enacting the deployment of TOSCA applications, which can be clustered in three main categories [1]. We can indeed distinguish (i) solutions for *directly deploying* TOSCA applications, (ii) approaches *integrating TOSCA with other standards* for enhancing deployment automation, and (iii) solutions for deploying TOSCA applications on *existing deployment technologies*. The reference approach for (i) is the OpenTOSCA engine proposed by Breitenbücher et al. [3]. OpenTOSCA enables directly deploying TOSCA applications on a target infrastructure, by requiring to get installed on a management node. OpenTOSCA is intended to be itself the orchestrator of the application, and it currently does not support streamlining the deployment of an application to other existing deployment technologies. Similar considerations apply to all other existing approaches for directly deploying TOSCA applications on target infrastructures [9]. All those approaches rely on the availability of full-fledged TOSCA-compliant orchestrators. In contrast, our objective is to enable deploying TOSCA applications by means of production-ready deployment technologies.

Efforts integrating TOSCA with other standards, i.e., concerning (ii), have been published by Calcaterra et al. [6] and Kopp et al. [14]. Both approaches integrate TOSCA with BPMN to imperatively program the deployment of multiservice applications. Additionally, Glaser et al. [11] proposes a cloud application orchestrator based on the integration of TOSCA with OCCI. However, despite the fact that the presented approaches enhance deployment automation by integrating TOSCA with existing standards, they still rely on the installation of some ad-hoc engine for processing the proposed solution.

Lastly, there are the solutions enabling the deployment of TOSCA applications on existing cloud deployment technologies. For instance, Breiter et al. [4] illustrate how to deploy TOSCA applications on the IBM cloud computing infrastructure. Brogi et al. [5] propose the TosKer engine for deploying and managing TOSCA applications on Docker-enabled infrastructures. Carrasco et al. [7] enable trans-cloud application deployment by allowing to run TOSCA application specifications on top of Apache Brooklyn. Additionally, Gusev et al. [12], Katsaros et al. [13] and Tricomi et al. [17] propose different approaches for deploying TOSCA applications on OpenStack cloud infrastructures. However, all these efforts target a precise cloud deployment technology. In contrast, our approach uses transformation and enables the deployment of TOSCA applications using the 13 most used production-ready deployment technologies, such as Terraform, Chef, or Puppet.

5   Conclusions

In this paper, we presented the open-source *TOSCA Lightning* toolchain, which enables the specification of multi-service applications in TOSCA, validating their compliance with TOSCA Light, and generating artifacts for enacting their deployment on 13 production-ready deployment technologies. We also presented an end-to-end case study illustrating how to exploit the *TOSCA Lightning* toolchain to specify the deployment of a third-party application and to automatically obtain the artifacts for effectively running the application with Kubernetes.

We plan to further evaluate TOSCA Light and the *TOSCA Lightning* toolchain in practice, by applying them to real-world industrial case studies. Further, as immediate future work, we plan to extend the TOSCA Lightning toolchain by a *Deployment Technology Integration Framework*. Based on the TOSCA Lightning transformation result, the goal is to directly trigger the automated deployment by unifying and encapsulating respective deployment technology APIs.

Acknowledgments. Work partially funded by projects *RADON* (EU, 825040), *SustainLife* (DFG, 379522012), and *DECLware* (Univ. of Pisa, PRA_2018_66).

References

1. Bellendorf, J., Mann, Z.A.: Specification of cloud topologies and orchestration using TOSCA: a survey. Computing **102**, 1793–1815 (2019). https://link.springer.com/article/10.1007/s00607-019-00750-3#citeas
2. Brabra, H., Mtibaa, A., Gaaloul, W., Benatallah, B., Gargouri, F.: Model-driven orchestration for cloud resources. In: 2019 IEEE International Conference on Cloud Computing (CLOUD), pp. 422–429 (2019)
3. Breitenbücher, U., et al.: The OpenTOSCA ecosystem - concepts & tools. In: European Space Project on Smart Systems, Big Data, Future Internet - Towards Serving the Grand Societal Challenges - Volume 1: EPS Rome 2016 (2016)
4. Breiter, G., et al.: Software defined environments based on TOSCA in IBM cloud implementations. IBM J. Res. Dev. **58**(2/3), 9:1–9:10 (2014)
5. Brogi, A., Rinaldi, L., Soldani, J.: TosKer: a synergy between TOSCA and Docker for orchestrating multicomponent applications. Softw. Pract. Exp. **48**(11), 2061–2079 (2018)
6. Calcaterra, D., Cartelli, V., Di Modica, G., Tomarchio, O.: A framework for the orchestration and provision of cloud services based on TOSCA and BPMN. In: Ferguson, D., Muñoz, V.M., Cardoso, J., Helfert, M., Pahl, C. (eds.) CLOSER 2017. CCIS, vol. 864, pp. 262–285. Springer, Cham (2018). https://doi.org/10.1007/978-3-319-94959-8_14

7. Carrasco, J., Durán, F., Pimentel, E.: Trans-cloud: CAMP/TOSCA-based bidimensional cross-cloud. Comput. Stand. Interfaces **58**, 167–179 (2018)
8. Chandrasekaran, A.: Gartner report: best practices for running containers and Kubernetes in production (2019)
9. Cloudify: TOSCA Orchestration & Training (2020). https://cloudify.co/tosca
10. Endres, C., et al.: Declarative vs. imperative: two modeling patterns for the automated deployment of applications. In: Proceedings of the 9th International Conference on Pervasive Patterns and Applications, pp. 22–27. Xpert Publishing Services (2017)
11. Glaser, F., Erbel, J., Grabowski, J.: Model driven cloud orchestration by combining TOSCA and OCCI. In: Proceedings of the 7th International Conference on Cloud Computing and Services Science - Volume 1: CLOSER, pp. 672–678. SciTePress (2017)
12. Gusev, M., Kostoska, M., Ristov, S.: Cloud P-TOSCA porting of N-tier applications. In: 2014 22nd Telecommunications Forum Telfor (TELFOR), pp. 935–938 (2014)
13. Katsaros, G., et al.: Cloud application portability with TOSCA, Chef and Openstack. In: 2014 IEEE International Conference on Cloud Engineering, pp. 295–302 (2014)
14. Kopp, O., Binz, T., Breitenbücher, U., Leymann, F.: BPMN4TOSCA: a domainspecific language to model management plans for composite applications. In: Mendling, J., Weidlich, M. (eds.) BPMN 2012. LNBIP, vol. 125, pp. 38–52. Springer, Heidelberg (2012). https://doi.org/10.1007/978-3-642-33155-8_4
15. Kopp, O., Binz, T., Breitenbücher, U., Leymann, F.: Winery – a modeling tool for TOSCA-based cloud applications. In: Basu, S., Pautasso, C., Zhang, L., Fu, X. (eds.) ICSOC 2013. LNCS, vol. 8274, pp. 700–704. Springer, Heidelberg (2013). https://doi.org/10.1007/978-3-642-45005-1_64
16. OASIS: TOSCA Simple Profile in YAML Version 1.3 (2019)
17. Tricomi, G., et al.: Orchestrated multi-cloud application deployment in OpenStack with TOSCA. In: 2017 IEEE International Conference on Smart Computing, pp. 1–6 (2017)
18. Wurster, M., et al.: The EDMM modeling and transformation system. In: Yangui, S., et al. (eds.) ICSOC 2019. LNCS, vol. 12019, pp. 294–298. Springer, Cham (2020). https://doi.org/10.1007/978-3-030-45989-5_26
19. Wurster, M., et al.: The essential deployment metamodel: a systematic review of deployment automation technologies. SICS Softw. Intensiv. Cyber Phys. Syst. (2019). https://link.springer.com/article/10.1007/s00450-019-00412-x
20. Wurster, M., et al.: TOSCA light: bridging the gap between the TOSCA specification and production-ready deployment technologies. In: Proceedings of the 10th International Conference on Cloud Computing and Services Science (CLOSER 2020), pp. 216–226. SciTePress (2020)

Author Index

Printed in the United States
By Bookmasters